Conclusion

I pray that this book has provided helpful insight into your God-given destiny. Whatever your destiny is, I know it is rich, fulfilling, and valuable to others. You are the only one who can bring it to pass. With God's help, your life will be full, and you will make a difference in the world around you. You are not here just to make a living. Be excited! Be enthused! You have a great destiny to live!

.....FULFILLING YOUR GOD GIVEN DESTINY

To find additional teaching material by
Casey and Wendy Treat, or to learn more about
Casey Treat Ministries, please visit the web site at:
www.CaseyTreat.com.

You may also write to them at:

P.O. Box 98800
Seattle, WA 98198
206-824-8188

....Fulfilling Your God Given Destiny

Casey Treat

Publishers Since 1798

THOMAS NELSON PUBLISHERS
Nashville • Atlanta • London • Vancouver

Published in Nashville, Tennessee by Thomas Nelson, Inc.

Library of Congress Cataloging-in-Publication Data

Treat, Casey.
Fulfilling your God-given destiny / by Casey Treat.
p. cm.
ISBN 13: 978-0-7852-2783-0
1. Christian life. I. Title
BV4501.2.T69 1995
248.4—dc20 95–1379
CIP

Printed in the United States of America
07 08 09 10 11 BVG 5 4 3 2 1

Dedication

There is one Scripture that is particularly easy for me to obey: "Rejoice with the wife of your youth" (Proverbs 5:18).

Wendy became a part of my life when I was twenty years old in Bible college. For more than thirty years she has been my best friend, counselor, and partner in ministry. Her insight, honesty, and discipline have provided great support and security for me. She is a mighty woman, loving wife, caring mother, and an anointed minister.

Contents

1

Getting Started

The word *destiny* brings many thoughts and questions to mind. It's almost a bit mystical. But I'm sure you agree that committed followers of God should be interested in their destiny. *Destiny,* in the sense that we will use the word, is an all-encompassing term. It is:

> *A course or path in life that includes both the God-given destination you are seeking at life's end and your own faith-filled journey toward that destination.*

This description of destiny differs from some others. There are those who believe one's destiny is an act of "fate" or a result of chance. They think they have *no control* over their life's course or outcome. But I am here to tell you that you do! You not only have a *choice,* but a *responsibility*.

The fact is that the Bible teaches both that God has planned a wonderful life and destiny for you and that you have a responsibility to discover and live it. Proverbs 16:9 says, "A man's heart plans his way, but the LORD directs his steps." We must do our part, and God will surely do His.

Our part is to discover and live in God's desired destiny for us. There is a goal He wants to help you accomplish. You can do this day by day, taking positive, God-pleasing steps. This book will help you.

Achieving your destiny is a process. It is somewhat like a halfback's job in a football game. His team starts on its own twenty-yard line. His destiny is the goal line, eighty yards away. But his immediate destiny is a first down, just ten yards away. As he gains yardage, he's achieving his destiny. But he won't achieve his ultimate destiny until he gets the ball all the way across that goal line and hears the fans cheer. Finally, if everything goes right, his team will win the game. Winning the game is what we all want and what God wants for us.

With practice, the halfback finds he develops a sense of *vision* for the field ahead. He looks down the field and anticipates a hit to avoid. He senses a hole in the line where he should cut. *Vision* is:

The ability to anticipate, imagine, or foresee experiences and developments that move you along destiny's course.

You will develop sharper vision as you walk the destiny course of your life. You will develop an ability to discriminate between things you want to achieve and things you should avoid.

Your picking up this book is likely a destiny step for you. I believe God will use this book to help you grow, to gain understanding and yardage toward your destiny goal line. You'll learn to look ahead and anticipate what you should accomplish *and* avoid for God's glory. You'll learn about traveling your destiny course.

Step by step, you can travel your destiny course. As you do, it can be said that you are "fulfilling your destiny"—you are making the trip! One day each of us will get to the end of our life's road. On that day, if we have taken God-guided steps along the way, we will hear, "Well done, good and faithful servant" (Matt. 25:23).

You win! On that day, having done what He set forth for you to do, you will have fulfilled—completely—your destiny course for life.

In one sense, those who love Jesus all share the same final destiny: it is holiness; without it, we cannot enter heaven. An important aspect of our destiny walk is becoming more like God.

Yet in another sense, we each have a particular destiny on earth that is beyond our shared call to holiness. This is *your* destiny in God. It is *your* God-given course of life, with all its challenges and accomplishments and hopes and dreams.

It *is* possible for a Christian to come to the end of life on earth not having fulfilled this God-given destiny and purpose. It *is* possible for a Christian to end up sitting on the bench of life or observing from the stands or running in circles at the fifty-yard line with his bell rung.

All our lives will end somewhere, at some destination. But that's not what I mean when I talk about destiny. My use of the word refers to the fullest possible life you can have in Christ, the one God foresaw before you were born, a life in which you score big and win the game. This is God's plan for your life. Anything else is second-rate. So from here on, when I talk about achieving your destiny, that's what I mean: traveling God's course and achieving the destination He has planned for you.

Through lack of knowledge, compromise, bad choices, laziness, or selfishness, we can die not having achieved our God-given destiny, not having realized our potential usefulness and holiness.

Knowing Your Destiny Will Be Life Changing

Before the foundation of the world, you were on God's mind. Before you were in your mother's mind, you were on God's mind. He knew your name, how tall you would be, your shoe size. He knew your wife or your husband. And the Bible says He chose you. According to the good counsel of His will, He established a destiny plan for your life.

The song "He Rescued Me" tells us that God knew and loved us before we knew anything about Him. And He planned a wonderful life for us. *Wow! God is good!* I'm not deciding my destiny. I'm just discovering it. I don't have to make it happen. I just have to let it happen. I just have to take the path that He prearranged and made ready for me to take.

> *For we are God's [own] handiwork (His workmanship), recreated in Christ Jesus, [born anew] that we may do those good works which*

> *God predestined (planned beforehand) for us, (taking paths which He prepared ahead of time) that we should walk in them—living the good life which He prearranged and made ready for us to live. (Eph. 2:10, Amplified)*

The Bible says God wrote your name in the Lamb's Book of Life before He created the earth. Imagine: Before He created the earth, He knew my name—Casey Douglas Treat. It's in the Book. My destiny was set before the foundation of the world. I get up every morning and say, "This is the day the Lord hath made. I will rejoice because I have a destiny."

There is confidence, there is boldness, there is joy in knowing God planned your life and destiny. Some of you think things just happen, that you're just bumping along. Such thinking will relegate you to a life of feeling bad about yourself. It will trap you in the quagmire of feeling like an accident of evolution. But when you know you have a divine destiny, you feel like a child of God. You have the confidence that you are who God says you are.

I was on a plane the other day, and as we experienced turbulence, the wings moved up and down. The seat-belt sign came on, and you could hear the passengers groaning in fear. I just sat there and said, "Smooth out, air!" I was working on my book, and I didn't have time for rough air. I wasn't worried. Why? Because I know I have a destiny, and I haven't accomplished it yet. Riding on that plane, I knew I had a tomorrow. That's not egocentric. That's not a fanatical way of thinking. It's reality. I have a destiny to fulfill. I have a tomorrow to get to. I'm not finished yet.

Think of it: Whatever happens in the economy, God has a plan for your life. Whatever happens in government, God has a plan for your life. Whatever happens in the natural realm, God saw it and He knew it and planned a great life for you. That kind of thinking will get you out of bed feeling good. It will put pep in your step. It will give you a reason to live another day. Yes, times may be difficult, but knowing you have a destiny in life can help keep you going.

I am adopted by God as a son, not as a slave but as a son. I serve God because I love Him, not because I'm afraid of Him. He

sees me as a son, not a servant. He has a great plan for my future. All I have to do is discover it and follow it!

Look at Paul. He was a man who knew his destiny. He was stoned and left for dead outside the town of Lystra. But Paul wasn't ready. He stood up and said, "I'm not finished yet." He kept right on preaching the Word. Later, the devil got him out in a ship and created a storm. The ship was split in half by the violent waves. Paul grabbed a board and floated to shore. Then he stood on the sand and said, "I'm not finished yet." When the Philippians threw him in the inner prison, God sent an earthquake and shook the prison. The doors flew open, Paul came walking out, and said, "I'm not finished yet." So they beat him with rods until he was near death. And he stood and was healed and said, "I'm not finished yet." Finally he had preached all over the world. He said, "Now I've finished my course. I've kept the faith. I'm ready to be offered up for my Lord." Paul knew his God-given destiny, and it gave him great purpose and a godly drive for living. More than that, he knew when his earthly mission was finished, so he could have peace at death too.

Wouldn't you like to have such knowledge? You can! You can have a sense of destiny and purpose in life that will make every day a joy to live, as it was for Paul. More than that, you can have peace when you reach the end, as Paul did, knowing you've finished the race.

This book is meant to help you get there—to that destiny of God-foreseen purpose and fulfillment. I have a great passion to see people be all that God created them to be. I burn with a desire to see people fulfill their destinies. At times it makes me difficult to get along with, and not the most easy-going person (as my wife, Wendy, and assistant, Randy, would be quick to testify). I'm not here to please you, but rather urge you toward your destiny. Someone has said that a sure way to accomplish nothing is to spend your life trying to please others. There will be some parts of this book that will not please you. They may even offend or anger you. Maybe a little heat under the collar will put a fire in your bones that will lift you to a higher level of life and fulfillment of your God-given destiny.

Do You Desire Your Destiny?

There are four reasons why you may not read to the end of this book:

1. You are not really concerned with your destiny.
2. You think that you already have the information you need to realize your destiny. (I thought I did when I was 19.)
3. You won't take time to get the information you need to pursue your destiny.
4. You're still looking for the easy way to fulfill your destiny (there isn't one).

My prayer is that you will have the desire to attain your destiny, will be open to receive information to identify it, will make the time to pursue it, and will take the only way—God's way—to fulfill it.

The truths and principles in this book are neither new nor original. But they are presented in a new way, and I believe they will have a fresh impact on your life. Nothing that is true is new. The principles of God can be applied to every aspect of life. They work in business, family, ministry, etc. Whether you believe them or not, they are the truths that makes things work. If you accept and practice them, you will prosper. If you reject and deny them, you will fail. We don't need a new revelation or a miraculous plan, just a fresh approach to the God-given and proven truths that bring fulfillment and success in life—spiritually, emotionally, physically, and financially.

Drastic Changes

As you read on you may think of things in your life that need to change. Don't do anything drastic. Many times the frustrations and limitations we feel don't require us to change everything, but rather to make adjustments in course. Consider this illustration:

You are on a ship sailing east on the Pacific Ocean. All your needs are met and although the journey is not easy, it is going

well. Along the way you begin to feel restless. You feel dissatisfied, and you begin to think about all the things you've done and the things you want to do. You start to wonder about the course of your life, how you've used your time and what you've accomplished. You begin to look into the future, where you are going and what you want to accomplish. As the days go by and you sail along, you decide you want to change your life and do something different. You have sorted out your priorities and discovered your destiny. You've read my book, and you're ready to fulfill your destiny! Don't jump overboard!

Unless you're in sin, a drastic change is likely not necessary for fulfilling your destiny. You could hinder God's plan if you try to change too much too soon. Stay on the ship. Think about your current course and identify a rational way to make the needed changes. Consider these options:

- It may be that your ship should continue in its current direction and reach the shore currently in your sights before altering course.
- God may be using current circumstances to train and prepare you for an upcoming leg of your journey.
- It may be that you should make a slight course adjustment at this time and prepare for major changes later.
- You may discover that your purpose for sailing is correct but you need to set out for a different port.
- You may want to sail to the originally planned port and then sell the boat.

There will be some right changes for you to make and some right steps to take, but don't jump overboard—don't drop out of school, quit your job, leave your spouse, or abandon your church. Let the Spirit of God guide you into all truth and help you along the way to your destiny. The providence of God has been working in your life up until this point, so don't throw it all away. It may be that you are right where God wants you to be and this book has come to keep you on course to destiny's next level. Make changes wisely and patiently as you follow your course of destiny.

2

My Testimony: An Example of Seeking Destiny

I remember waking up in the county jail one morning thinking, "How did I get here?" The day before, I had used drugs on the way home from work. The next thing I knew, I was looking around the jail cell. It was a familiar sight. Though only nineteen, I'd been in jail six or seven times. Now, as I tried to piece together how this had happened again, I seemed to have developed temporary amnesia: I couldn't remember what I had done to land myself back behind bars. Clearly, I was once a person who had no sense of my God-given destiny.

Talking to the jailer and my attorney, I learned that while walking home from work, I had lost consciousness and fallen into a ditch. Someone driving by had seen me and called the police. When the police found me, I was still unconscious. They searched my pockets and, finding drugs, took me to jail.

That circumstance parallels so many that I found myself in as a young man. I'd look around and say, "How did I get here? This is not the life I want. These are not the circumstances I want. This is not the kind of person I want to be." I'd find myself in some of the most terrible situations and not know how I got into them or how to get out of them. When we have no sense of destiny, we usually end up in the ditch of life.

In Mark 5, Jesus heals a man who had been demon-possessed for some time. He had tried to kill himself and had abused and hurt himself. He ended up living in caves and screaming in pain and agony. Finally the Lord met him and cast the devil out of him. He returned to his right mind and was healed and restored. Grateful, he wanted to follow Jesus.

In Mark 5:19, Jesus said to the man, "Go home to your friends, and tell them what great things the Lord has done for you, and how He has had compassion on you." And the man did. He departed for the Decapolis, where he proclaimed all that Jesus had done for him. He was on the course to his destiny.

That's what I want to do. I want to share with you the great things the Lord has done for me and how He has had compassion on me. I want to show you how God revealed my destiny to me, so you can learn to see your own destiny. God wants to restore, heal, and deliver. He wants to show compassion toward every one of us. He wants to bring us into our right mind and into the happy and blessed life that living out our destiny brings.

In the next few pages, I want you to get to know who I was before I knew God and His destiny for me, and before I began walking on destiny's course. Then, in Chapter 11, after I've explained more fully the principles of destiny, we'll return to my life to help you put things together. You will then see how I became aware of my destiny and began to walk in it.

Growing up, I got good grades in school. I played sports and did the things that other boys were doing in my neighborhood. I had a good family. My mother and father gave me everything they could give me. They were not born again, so I was raised like an average American boy, not in a Christian family but nonetheless one that instilled a certain moral lifestyle.

I can remember at the early age of six wondering if anybody liked me—if I was important. I wanted to be accepted and received, and at that young age I began to do things to try to get people to like me. In addition to sports, I was into music. I played the organ, the piano, the drums, and the clarinet. Music brought me the acceptance and love I needed.

Being socially active and having a girlfriend were the highest priorities in my junior-high years. School was secondary. I went to school to meet people and have friends. Everything else in life

was unimportant. My driving force was feeding my need to be accepted, to be important, to be special. I looked for all this in a sexual relationship. Eventually I broadened my search to other areas—smoking cigarettes, drinking alcohol, and partying. By the time I was in the ninth grade, I was using drugs, smoking pot, and doing other things I said I would never do. I even became a drug dealer. Everybody wanted to talk to me. Everybody wanted to see me or call me. I was *the man with the plan*, so I became important—at least that's what I thought.

I didn't know that God had created me—that I was fearfully and wonderfully made. Because I didn't know God's Word, I didn't know that I was made in His likeness and image and that He loved me and had a destiny plan for my life. So I had to find a reason, a purpose for living. I tried to find that purpose in drugs and in relationships.

In my late teens, my mother and father's relationship began to break up. This was tragic for me, because I'd seen friends whose parents had divorced and I made statements like, "I'm glad that will never happen to me. Wouldn't that be terrible if your dad or mom left?" I remember feeling the pain of Mom and Dad's separation and seeing Mom with a boyfriend and Dad with a girlfriend. I came to the conclusion then that there must be no right or wrong. I said to myself, "Well, hey, I guess it's every man for himself. It's anything goes. If it feels good, do it."

After my graduation from high school in 1973, I started getting arrested. The first time was at my class's senior party. The police found me with drugs, and I was taken to jail. That was a scary situation, but fear and the threat of jail will not motivate you to change if you're hurting inside. All this time I never told anyone I was hurting. I wouldn't admit to a need of any kind. I wanted to be cool. I was trying to be popular and involved with the in crowd.

Drugs became my driving force. I was addicted. Of course, I always wanted a girlfriend close by to make me feel like a real man. I wanted a sexual relationship to make me feel important. Yet my relationships were shallow, and in many ways that added to the pain, because I knew they weren't real. I didn't want to hurt people, but I often ended up using them anyway.

The number of arrests increased. One day, while driving on the interstate, I blacked out and veered into the median. The ground was very wet, as it so often is here in the Northwest, so my car bogged down in the mud. I just sat there spinning my wheels for I don't know how long. I could have burned an entire tank of gas for all I know.

I sat there with my foot on the accelerator, tires spinning, mud flying everywhere. Coming to, I thought, "Be cool, man. Don't attract any attention to yourself. You don't want to get arrested again. You haven't even gone to court for the last charges!"

The next thing I remember is seeing flashing lights and hearing the police officer yelling, "Shut the car off! Shut the car off!" It was only then I realized that I wasn't even on the road but in the median throwing mud fifty feet into the air.

I wonder how many people are sitting in the median of their lives not going north or south, just stuck in the mud. Their wheels are spinning, and they're making a lot of noise and displacing a lot of dirt, but they're not going anywhere. That was the reality of my life. I was just sitting there, kicking up mud and going nowhere. I had no sense of God, no sense of my God-given destiny.

The police took me in and gave me a sobriety test. I hadn't had any alcohol. Then they checked my blood and, of course, I was loaded on drugs, all kinds of drugs. So back into jail I went. This was happening so often that I couldn't even get to court on the former charges. They'd just keep adding more charges to my record.

There I was, only nineteen years old, addicted to drugs and miserable. Instead of being excited with a vision for my destiny in life, I was hoping I wouldn't have to go to prison. Instead of looking forward to college and building a career, or looking for a wife and starting a family, I was trying to stay loaded and keep myself out of jail.

I began to feel afraid, and I realized that I was no longer able to control my behavior or my circumstances. I feared I was going to die young and that would be the end of it. Then I began to think maybe that would be better—just get this thing over with, because I didn't see too many happy people around me.

My parents weren't any happier than I was. By that time my mom had been diagnosed with multiple sclerosis and was trying to cope with that dreaded disease and the recent divorce. My dad was just trying to earn a living. Everybody around me was doing the same thing I was doing—just trying to get by. Were there any happy people in the world? I began to seriously contemplate suicide.

Then the courts began to work with me. They sent me to a drug-and-alcohol counselor, a doctor, and a psychiatrist. Most of them drank and smoked, so I knew they weren't any better off than I was. You can't fool worldly drug users. You can't con them or play games with them. They've played all the games, and they know all the cons. I realized right away that most of these people didn't have anything to offer me.

Finally the probation office sent me for counseling to the Washington Drug Rehabilitation Center (WDRC), which was founded by a man named Julius Young. He talked to me about my behavior and lifestyle. He confronted me with the results of my thinking and actions, and he challenged me to change. He was hard, but he had a life and strength that I wanted. I became excited about the possibility of a new life.

My mom had bailed me out of jail and told me I had to pay her back by going to church. (By this time she had been born again.) So I went to church, but the preacher had no life and no power. The congregation sang a couple of slow hymns and said a prayer. I didn't find any life there, and I walked out thinking, "These people are no better off than I am."

I ended up loaded again, and this time I didn't even know where I was. I had come home, gotten out of the car, gone in the house, and passed out on the bed. I didn't realize that I'd forgotten to shut the car off and put it in park. Mom looked out the window, and my car was rolling across the yard. It came to rest against the barn and sat there idling. Mom walked outside to the barn, and there was my car still running. I was caught!

She came in and tried to wake me but couldn't—I was stone gone. When she called my probation officer, he said, "This is the last straw," and enrolled me in the Washington Drug Rehabilitation Center. The program has since closed, but at that time it

was the most powerful and effective program for drug users in the Northwest and possibly on the West Coast.

I started the program the next day, a bit scared and nervous. It was a residential program, and I was to be there for at least a year. But I figured I would get it together in a couple of months, and they'd let me go because I was such a sharp guy. I wasn't supposed to take any of my possessions with me, but I managed to smuggle in some drugs. I thought, "Hey, I don't want to give up drugs completely. I'll just get enough control of my life so I can go to work and pay my bills." I really didn't think I needed to stop using drugs.

But at the WDRC, I found a group of people who were fired up! They were excited! They were moving fast and working hard. At that time I didn't know they were all born again and filled with the Holy Spirit.

I soon found out this place was tough. It was like a military discipleship program. The probation officer had said to me, "You've got a choice. You can either go into this program, or you can take your chances with the judge and see how long he will give you in the state penitentiary."

I said, "Hey, I'll take the program." And so I went in not really planning to change, just intending to get a little bit better so I could control myself. But I found a lifestyle that was so exciting that I fell in love with it. That's where I really learned who Jesus is and what the Christian life is all about. These people were living the Word of God in a way that I'd never seen before. I wanted that kind of life!

In about two weeks I went to the director's office and told him, "You know, I've had these drugs in my clothes. I smuggled them in." Then I poured all the drugs down the toilet. "I really want to change," I said.

That was the beginning of a new life for me. A couple of months later I was born again and started going to church. Then I was baptized in water and baptized in the Holy Spirit. I began to pray in other tongues, and the power of God started to flow in my life. At that point, I was definitely on the way to my destiny. But I had just begun.

I was a resident of WDRC for almost two years. Then I was a staff member for a couple of years. During that time I enrolled in

ministry training school, and after four years I received my bachelor of theology degree. It was at school that I met Wendy, who would become my wife.

In my years with WDRC, thousands of people came into the program, and only thirty graduated. Those who did learned how to discipline themselves and how to live the Word of God. That program laid the foundation for the ministry that the Lord has given me today. The Word of God really works! It produces good fruit! So many Christians struggle because they haven't had the discipleship or training of a solid foundation.

It was during that time that I learned about renewing the mind—the message God has given me to share with the world. People call me or write to me weekly saying, "Would you come and teach about change and renewing the mind? Tell us how your life has been changed." The truth of renewing the mind, found in Romans 12:2 and throughout all the books of the New Testament, is the key to Christian growth.

At WDRC I learned how to control my thoughts—how to transform the thoughts of depression into thoughts of faith and excitement. I learned how to take thoughts of worldliness and desire for drugs and sex and transform them into thoughts of holiness, righteousness, and a desire for God. As Paul urges in 2 Corinthians 10:5, I learned how to capture my thoughts and make them obedient to the Word of God—to control what was going on in my mind so I could control what was going on in my life.

I also learned how to build relationships. We are members of the same body, and when a body has members that don't work well together, that body is weak and dysfunctional.

As I worked with others, as I ministered, as I studied and prayed, the course of my destiny became clearer. I discovered that the longer you walk the path of your destiny, the better you become acquainted with it. (In the last chapter of this book, you'll see just how my sense of destiny in God crystallized.) But right now, suffice it to say that after teaching a weekly Bible study of about forty people in 1978 and 1979, in January of 1980 we started Christian Faith Center in South Seattle in a rented foyer off a school gymnasium. I was on the radio for fifteen minutes a day

at that time. Today Christian Faith Center averages six thousand people every week.

Within the past couple of years I've been in many different countries—Zimbabwe, Australia, Germany, Bulgaria, South Africa, the Philippines, Korea, Hong Kong, Wales, all over the United States and Canada. We've only just begun. We're going to minister all over the world. Our books and tapes are going into many nations and have been translated into several different languages. The number will increase in coming years. We believe our church will continue to grow until Jesus comes. Our growth is based on knowing our God-given destiny and living it out.

God wants to use you in some special way. Maybe you won't be a pastor or Bible teacher, but in some way you can influence, bless, and make a difference in your world. I have been used by God to the same extent that I have been able to discern and realize my destiny. You can do the same. You can go from someone going nowhere, like I was, to someone with an exciting destiny.

But before you can make a difference, before you can discover your God-given destiny, you must be born of the Spirit and filled with the Spirit. If that's where you already are, then wonderful! We'll have fun exploring this book's principles together. But if you haven't yet been born again, I encourage you to pray in faith and sincerity this simple prayer:

> *Jesus, forgive me of my sins. I ask You to come into my life and be my Lord. I believe You died for me and You were then raised from the dead. I turn from my ways to Your ways. I thank You that You will now show me the great destiny You have for me. Amen.*

If you prayed that prayer and meant it, then God has surely heard you and saved you! You can now join the rest of us as we consider how to discover our wonderful God-given destiny.

Recently I went to talk with the judge who sentenced me fifteen years ago. I asked him why he hadn't put me in prison. He said, "I felt there was hope for you. I wanted to give you a chance."

I began to tell him what happened to me, how I had been born again. I told him how I had earned a degree in theology. I told him about starting a church and how the church had grown. I

told him how we have opened Dominion College, which trains college students to be leaders in business, ministry, and education.

The judge looked at me and said, "My goodness! Thank God you made it! Thank God you changed! I hear so few positive reports. It's exciting to hear someone who really made it through the system and got into a good life."

The world doesn't have many answers for people who are hurting. It doesn't have much help to offer. The judges are not going to make a difference in our world. The courts and prisons are not going to make a difference. But if we'll get right with God and then get a sense of God's destiny for us individually and collectively, there's no limit to how He can use us. There's nothing that can hold us back.

You too can have God's will, His plan, His abundance in every realm of your life. You can experience His destiny for your life. My story began when a young drug user wanted to change his life. How did I discover my destiny and start maximizing my potential? The same way you can. Just read on. Your story begins here.

3

How to Discover Your Destiny

- How do I know God's will for my life?
- How do I know my gifts and calling?
- How can I find a career that will satisfy my desires?

So many people go through life unhappy with their careers and their lifestyle because they have never found the answers to these questions. You will find the answers in the following chapters. God really does have a plan for your life, and you can know what it is. The bottom line is: *God has a destiny that He planned for you and you alone, a wonderful, God-glorifying, fulfilling life of joy.*

When you understand God's purposes for your life, you will enter into the greatest joy and peace possible.

> *Just as He chose us in Him before the foundation of the world, that we should be holy and without blame before Him in love, having predestined us to adoption as sons by Jesus Christ to Himself, according to the good pleasure of His will. (Eph. 1:4-5)*

> *For we are His workmanship, created in Christ Jesus for good works, which God prepared beforehand that we should walk in them. (Eph. 2:10)*

Before I formed you in the womb I knew you;
Before you were born I sanctified you;
I ordained you a prophet to the nations. (Jer. 1:5)

For You formed my inward parts;
You covered me in my mother's womb.
I will praise You, for I am fearfully and wonderfully made;
Marvelous are Your works,
And that my soul knows very well. (Ps. 139:13-14)

Your eyes saw my substance, being yet unformed.
And in Your book they all were written,
The days fashioned for me,
When as yet there were none of them. (Ps. 139:16)

The omniscience of God goes beyond time, space, and all human limitations. God sees every day as if it were today. Yesterday, today, and tomorrow are all the same to Him. Before He created the earth, He saw you and He knew you. He knew your strengths and weaknesses, your gifts and talents. He knew the choices you would make, the things you would desire and the things that would fulfill your life. With that knowledge, God established a purpose and a plan for your existence. He established your destiny.

DESTINY KEY

GOD REALLY DOES HAVE A DESTINY PLAN FOR YOUR LIFE AND YOU CAN KNOW WHAT IT IS.

The circumstances surrounding your birth may not have been ideal. Your mother may not have wanted a child. Your father may not have been there for you. But God knew you and predetermined a purpose for you. In the minds of men, you may have been an *accident*. But in the mind of God you were planned, wanted, predestined to be a part of His family.

But predestination does not remove personal choices and willpower from your life. It is important for you to realize that all of God's plans are based on foreknowledge. Romans 8:29 says, "For whom He foreknew, He also predestined." That means that because God knows you, your desires and your choices, He can

plan accordingly. We are not puppets on a string. Our will is a part of God's plan.

> *I call heaven and earth as witnesses today against you, that I have set before you life and death, blessing and cursing; therefore choose life, that both you and your descendants may live. (Deut. 30:19)*

God takes the knowledge of your choices and makes them a part of His plan for you. He foreknew your choices, but He still left you with the right to choose. For instance, He saw the person you would choose to marry. Based on that choice, God planned a destiny for you that will work within your marriage. He has led you, influenced you, and directed your steps when you didn't even know it. That is why you shouldn't say, "I married the wrong person," or "God had another spouse for me." Once you have chosen, that person becomes a part of God's plan for you. To use football terminology, the two of you need to learn how to block for each other and to carry and pass the ball so you can work your way down the playing field of life.

Seeds in the Early Years

The book of Proverbs says, "Train up a child in the way he should go, and when he is old he will not depart from it" (Prov. 22:6). This could also read, "in the way he should *not* go." Many of us struggle as adults because of ideals, philosophies, and untruths that were instilled in us as children.

One of the greatest tragedies in public schools today is the teaching of the theory of evolution as if it were fact. I remember as a young person seeing an illustration on the wall showing animals growing into other forms, eventually becoming monkeys, and then "evolving" into man. This was presented as fact, and for years I believed that it was a scientific reality. Even without biblical knowledge, we know that the theory of evolution is more myth and fantasy than science and fact. The fact is that it takes more faith to believe in evolution than it does to believe in a God who created the world.

The result of evolutionary teaching is that students believe there is no purpose or reason for their existence. They are accidents of nature. There was no plan for man—just a mutation in nature that brought us to our present form. We have no purpose, so we have no destiny.

With that mentality, young people come to believe that there are no absolutes. Everything is a product of natural accident, so sex before marriage can't be wrong, using drugs can't be wrong, being homosexual can't be wrong. There is no right and wrong, because we are all evolutionary animals anyway. The moral failure, the marriage failure, and the family failure of America are due in part to the removal from school of the truth about God and His plan for every life.

If I have no reason for existence, then I will have no self-esteem. Low self-esteem causes people to treat themselves and those around them in a negative way. If my ancestor was an ape, then humankind is an accident and a mutation. So I might as well do whatever feels good, because my life has no purpose anyway.

The lack of self-worth in people today goes back to the teaching they received (or didn't receive) as children. Historically, American schools and families taught that God created man for a reason and that if we would seek the Lord and choose to live right, we would find that reason and have a good life. Even when life was hard there was a sense that it had meaning and we would learn more as we went along. There was a sense of destiny and purpose, and we were on a mission to discover it.

Consider this example: What good is a car if no one knows its purpose? In such a case, a car would have no value. We might admire it as a sculpture piece or use it as a camp in the backyard, but we would not be able to enjoy all that it was designed for—transporting us from one place to another. It would not fulfill the purpose its creator intended. So it is for you and me. What good are we if we don't know what we were created for—our purpose and destiny?

When we lack the knowledge of the Creator's purpose in bringing us into the world, we live far below that purpose. But when we know our destiny, we can rise to it and be all that we were created to be.

When all sense of destiny and purpose is removed, restraint, values, self-esteem, and self-worth disappear. We're left with a void, which we try to fill with sex, drugs, alcohol, and other stimulants. In our schools at Christian Faith Center, our top priority is to fill young people with the knowledge of God, who knew them and predestined them before they were born. Then they have a basis for discipline and values, and they have a mission in life.

I was taught at a young age that there was a mysterious force called *fate*. I didn't know what or who fate was, but I thought it was the reason things happened. When my mother was diagnosed as having multiple sclerosis, or when my parents were divorced, or when my grandfather died, I was told it was just fate.

This left me with the feeling that I was at the mercy of a mysterious force I could not control. I might not have a good marriage or happy children or a long life because "you never know what fate might do."

This "fatalistic" philosophy produces poor self-esteem and a negative lifestyle, because like evolution it rejects a loving God and denies the fact that my life has a plan, a purpose, and a destiny.

Things do not happen because of fate. In fact, there are five causes of incidents in our lives:

1. God influences, leads, and directs us.
2. Satan comes to kill, steal, and destroy.
3. Other people make decisions and actions that affect me.
4. I make decisions and carry out those decisions.
5. Natural, physical incidents in the world impact us.

How Do I Know What God Has Planned for My Life?

> *Blessed be the God and Father of our Lord Jesus Christ, who has blessed us with every spiritual blessing in the heavenly places in Christ . . . to the praise of the glory of His grace, by which He made us accepted in the Beloved. . . . That in the dispensation of*

the fullness of the times He might gather together in one all things in Christ, both which are in heaven and which are on earth—in Him. In Him also we have obtained an inheritance, being predestined according to the purpose of Him who works all things according to the counsel of His will. (Eph. 1:3, 6, 10-11)

These verses and many others make it clear that God knew us before we were born and has a plan for our life. And if this is true, there must be a way for us to know what that plan is. God does not expect us to live in a state of confusion. He doesn't want us to go through life making "trial-and-error" attempts at finding our destiny. God created us to be intelligent, thoughtful, planning, envisioning creatures. Therefore He can and will communicate with us if we desire to hear Him and follow Him. Jesus said that everyone who asks receives; everyone who seeks finds; to everyone who knocks, the door will be opened. If you truly desire to know your destiny, you can know it.

DESTINY KEY

GOD CREATED US TO BE INTELLIGENT, THOUGHTFUL, PLANNING, ENVISIONING PEOPLE.

This chapter offers not a formula or a scientific plan, but rather a series of steps that will bring you to an awareness of your course in life. One step alone will not bring this awareness, but taken together they will light the way so you can begin to see your destiny unfold.

Even after twenty years of walking on my course of destiny, I continue to learn new aspects of God's plan. When I first became a Christian, I had a very limited sense of my destiny. By the time I started Christian Faith Center, my destiny was clearer. Today it is even more apparent. Greater avenues of adventure open up to me as I go along. We don't need to have the whole picture clear in our mind all at once. If all we understand clearly is our next step, we should take that step. After all, our first step was to accept Christ as our Savior and Lord. Since then, we've taken other steps on our course of destiny. God will always bring us to the next step at His chosen time.

As I look back over the various stages of development in my destiny, I realize that if God had shown me the whole picture, I would have been afraid to move; in human terms, I would have "messed it up" with premature action (or should I say immature action?).

Ten Key Questions That Will Uncover Your Destiny

1. What is the deepest desire of your heart?

In Psalm 37:4 we read:

Delight yourself also in the LORD,
And He shall give you the desires of your heart.

I see two truths in this verse: (1) As I delight in knowing and serving God, He places desires within me. He causes me to desire those things that are in His plan for my life. (2) As I delight in knowing and serving God, He gives me the things I desire. Natural things and spiritual things are granted to me. Just as a father on earth desires to give good gifts to his children, so our heavenly Father desires to give good gifts to His children.

Some religions try to teach us that desires are wrong or evil and should be denied or suppressed. Many who were raised in church feel guilty for having desires and would never expect God to fulfill them. This is one of the reasons why many people leave the church. They aren't able to deal with the conflict of having desires and feeling guilty about them.

Desire is not only God-given, it is part of the development of destiny in our lives. The young man who loves to talk and cannot be quiet in class may someday communicate truths that will change the lives of his listeners. The young woman who loves to tell everyone what to do and take control of every situation may someday manage and govern the lives of people.

I recall a conversation with a man in our church about the "evils" of desire. He had been raised in a church that taught that whatever he desired was probably of the flesh or from the devil. In fact, he thought the thing that he really didn't want to do was

probably what God wanted him to do. In his mind his destiny was found in the thing that he despised most. By doing what he didn't really want to do, he felt he was being more "spiritual."

Fred Price, pastor of Crenshaw Christian Center in Los Angeles, once said, "It is hard enough for God to get people to be productive Christians by calling them to do what they truly desire. It would be next to impossible to get them to produce good fruit by doing things they don't desire." I've actually had people say to me, "I don't want to make Jesus Lord of my life because He might tell me to go to Africa and be a missionary, and I don't want to go."

DESTINY KEY

DESIRE IS NOT ONLY A GOD-GIVEN CAPACITY, IT IS PART OF THE DEVELOPMENT OF DESTINY IN OUR LIVES.

God doesn't work that way. Desire is a God-given force that He uses to help us fulfill our destiny. I'm not saying that we are under some form of control by God. He has given us a free will. But God knows our personality, our gifts, and our talents. He uses those things and causes us to desire experiences that offer great excitement, fulfillment, and satisfaction.

But what is a "desire"? We all have had whims, fantasies, and wishes throughout our life. *These are not desires, but passing thoughts.* The little boy wants to be a baseball player, a fireman, and a policeman all in the same day. He is "trying on" his dreams and learning to distinguish his desires from his fantasies. As parents we can help him sort out all these things. Fantasies come and go, but desires last a lifetime.

The desire you feel to speak, to sing, to create, to manage, or to build is there because God placed it there. As you separate your deep, heartfelt desires from your fantasies and ideas, you will be drawn to study and prepare to do those things. The number-one question asked of a college student is, "What do you want to do?" Everyone knows that your desire is linked to your destiny.

Desire, as God created it, is a positive power. You will discover your destiny as you clarify the things you *really* want.

2. What stirs your passion?

Passion is that zeal, fire, excitement, and intensity that you feel about things that are important to you. Passion is powerful. In John 2:15 Jesus cleansed the temple. He drove out the animals and money changers and overturned their tables because they had made the house of God a den of thieves. The disciples then remembered the verse from Psalm 69:9—"Zeal for Your house has eaten me up." Jesus was consumed with such passion for the sacredness of the house of God that he became violent.

Passion stirs us to action. It causes us to "do something." A passion for song, praise, and worship motivates us to learn, to practice, and to bring forth the music God has put in our heart. A passion for children motivates us to reach out to young ones, to bring them up in the nurture and admonition of the Lord. A passion for building stirs us to be concerned with the smallest detail of construction, making sure everything is done perfectly. A passion for numbers may lead us to accounting. A passion for words inspires us to write. Some people have a passion for helping others. They may become nurses, social workers, or counselors. Still others have a passion for persuasion, and they go into sales.

DESTINY KEY

PASSION IS THAT ZEAL, FIRE, EXCITEMENT, AND INTENSITY THAT YOU FEEL ON THE INSIDE TOWARD THINGS THAT ARE IMPORTANT TO YOU.

One of the ways we can know our destiny is by answering the question, "What makes me the most upset?" If we care to the point of anger about something, it may be a part of our heart. There are some things that we couldn't care less about, but that other people are passionate about. There are things that *we* become stirred up about but that other people don't even notice. It all comes down to your passion.

The evangelist can't stand thinking of lost souls dying and going to hell. He feels that money spent on anything but evangelism is a waste. The pastor sees hurting Christians and can't

stand the thought of them wandering without a church, without teaching and counseling. He gives himself to the cause that stirs his passion, because that is his destiny.

Many great enterprises, businesses, ministries, schools, and movements have been started because of someone's anger. Mothers Against Drunk Drivers (MADD) was birthed by a mother who was enraged by the number of alcohol-related traffic accidents in America. Her anger led her to a destiny that has helped many people and saved many lives.

Lester Sumrall's Feed the Hungry program took root when he thought about God's people praying "give us this day our daily bread" while many people still suffered from hunger, and this image would not leave his mind. His compassion and pain drove him to his destiny.

Schools have been founded by teachers who could not stand the plight of underprivileged children in the city. Businesses have been launched because someone was frustrated by inferior service from existing companies. All these things show the power of passion.

There is something that stirs your passion. Is it a desire to see the office work done more efficiently? To have people communicating more clearly? To hear truth being taught? To change a part of your city? The desires in your heart offer clues to the destiny in your life. Discover your passion! It runs through you like a stream. Perhaps now it is a small trickle, but with time, it can become a great river! What motivates you to do something? What will you argue about, get stirred about, be upset about? That is a clue to your destiny.

Remember, we are discovering, not deciding our destiny.

> *A man's steps are of the LORD;*
> *How then can a man understand his own way? (Prov. 20:24)*

3. What flows naturally out of you?

Your course of destiny will feel right—will feel natural—as you discover it. People who have found their place in God's plan are doing what is natural to them. Although it is exciting, challenging, and inspiring, there is also a sense of naturalness about it. It seems "right"; it just "flows." Walking your God-given course

will be like striding in the pair of shoes that fits perfectly, sitting in the cozy chair that feels better than any other, wearing your favorite jacket. It may be too big or too small for others, but to you it is just right.

That can be part of the problem in the minds of some people. They keep looking for something special, something unique and out of the ordinary. They ignore the things they do best. They avoid the things that come naturally. They keep trying to come up with something difficult. They try to squeeze on that size eight even though they are a size ten.

> ***DESTINY KEY***
>
> PEOPLE WHO HAVE FOUND THEIR GOD-GIVEN DESTINY ARE DOING WHAT IS NATURAL TO THEM.

I went to Bible school with a man named Terry Tarsiuk. He became one of my best friends and a fellow minister. He tried for years to become a pastor and to start his own church. We had trained together for that purpose, and we both set out to make it happen. Terry was a great pianist and songwriter. I always wondered why he didn't develop that area of ministry further. Several years after college, Terry came to be a part of Christian Faith Center as he prepared to start a new church in Canada. After some time he became a leader in our music ministry and had a profound impact on our church. Finally his wife and others began to challenge him on what he was really called to do. We all sensed the great impact his music ministry was having on people, but he didn't see it.

To Terry, music was too easy. He'd played the piano all his life. But finally he began to feel a sense of destiny about it. He realized everything he really wanted to give to people was happening via his music ministry. He didn't need to start a church. In fact, many aspects of pastoring weren't even exciting or interesting to him. He soon changed his course and has become a part of our leadership team. His ministry has touched thousands of people, and he is a great blessing around the world.

Terry almost missed his God-given destiny, because he was so close to it. It was too natural and normal to him. He had grown up knowing he was called to the ministry, and to him that meant

he was to be a pastor. That was the direction he was heading. But God had called him to something else. When you hear Terry tell of this process today, you'll hear him thank God (and his wife) that he plugged in to his real destiny. Pastoring would not have been successful for him—at least not as successful as his music ministry is now.

Romans 12:4-6 says:

> *For as we have many members in one body, but all the members do not have the same function, so we, being many, are one body in Christ, and individually members of one another. Having then gifts differing according to the grace that is given to us, let us use them.*

Terry is now using his gifts and performing the function for which he was designed. He is living out his destiny! God has given you grace to do what He has gifted you to do. With the gift comes the grace. Whatever part of His body you are, your function will flow naturally, because you have the grace for it. Your feet are designed to stand and walk; they have what it takes to do their job without difficulty. You can walk on your hands and knees, but it isn't natural, efficient, or comfortable. Your hands don't have the grace for walking, but your feet do. Every part of your physical body has a natural function.

Similarly, you are a part of the body of Christ. There is a place where you will function in the church and the world without strain. You have the grace and the gifts to get the job done. Doing your job will be easy. Not that you don't have to work and apply yourself. Your feet do get tired. But there will be a natural feeling about what you are doing.

Teaching, preaching, working with leaders, managing money, building new buildings feels so good to me because that is my function. People have asked me, "Aren't you going crazy with all these activities? How do you handle the pressure?" To me it is not pressure; it is a joy. I have the grace and the gifts to perform my duties as a pastor because this is my destiny. Your *calling* is:

The specific thing you do—a career or job or ministry in which God has placed you as you seek to accomplish a purpose, fulfill a vision, and complete your course of destiny.

A teacher can handle twenty-five active minds and bodies, the builder can decipher complex blueprints, and the salesman can handle resistant customers because that is their calling. It is their destiny!

Find what flows naturally—what feels normal. This is likely your calling on the road of destiny. It may be big or small; the size of the task doesn't matter. You may think it's easy, but to others it would be hard! If the shoe fits, wear it, and stop looking for your destiny in the wrong places.

4. Where do you bring forth fruit or produce good results?

"A tree is known by its fruit" (Matt. 12:33). If it's God's plan, a tree will be fruitful and productive.

Jesus told a parable of an orchard with a fig tree that wasn't bearing fruit (Luke 13:6-9). The owner gave the orchard keeper one year to make it productive. If it didn't bring forth fruit, he said, "Cut it down; why does it use up the ground?" God isn't interested in things that don't work. If you've been leading a church for ten years and have twenty-five people, I'd say you are not on your destiny course (unless there are only fifty people in your town).

If your business isn't making a profit you must make a change. "Fertilize it" and make whatever adjustments would be appropriate to turn it around. But if profits still don't come after a reasonable amount of time, close the business down and get on with something productive.

In Matthew 25, we learn that God was upset with the man who hid his talent and didn't earn any interest on it. In fact, He threw him into outer darkness, where there is weeping and gnashing of teeth. The two men who produced a profit, whatever the size, were blessed and invited into the joy of the Lord. God is a pragmatist. If it doesn't work, it's probably not in His plan for you to do it. Too many Christians waste their lives doing things

that are irrelevant and unproductive. You owe it to yourself and your Lord to be fruitful and productive.

The exciting thing about your destiny is that it was designed in the counsel of God's will (Eph. 1:11). He created you for a purpose. God had a person or people that He needed to affect in some way. And so you were born. It's not that you were born and then God came up with something for you to do. God had something for you to do before the foundation of the world. You were born to do it. Your purpose was established—then your existence was established. God has a productive life planned for you, a life of meaning and purpose that will make a difference in others' lives and in His kingdom. It may be to affect one person or family who then go on to affect many others. It may be to raise great kids and then help other parents do the same. (What a tremendous need in today's world!) It may be to assist someone who is touching other lives and to help make that ministry or business a success.

DESTINY KEY

GOD PLANNED FOR EVERY ONE OF US TO BRING FORTH GOOD FRUIT THROUGHOUT OUR LIFETIME.

God wants everyone to:

- Have a long healthy life (Ps. 91:16);
- Have good marriage/family relationships (Gen. 1:28; 2:18);
- Show financial generosity (Prov. 3:9-10);
- Have a positive influence on other people (Matt. 22:39).

One thing you should know for sure: God has not planned a barely-get-by, mediocre, mundane life for you. It is not part of God's character to bring someone into the world for no purpose. He has never created anyone for no reason or for an evil purpose. There are times of struggle and despair in every life. There are times of sowing and times of reaping. We all go through winters before we enjoy the summer, but God

planned for every one of us to bring forth good fruit throughout our lifetime.

God is a good shepherd, not an evil one. If we walk with Him we shall not want. There will be valleys that we go through—even the valley of the shadow of death. But He will not leave us there. We never camp in the valley. We go through it to reach our destiny.

5. What is the witness of the Holy Spirit in your spirit?

> *For as many as are led by the Spirit of God, these are sons of God. . . . The Spirit Himself bears witness with our spirit that we are children of God. (Rom. 8:14, 16)*

God has a way of letting us know what is right, what is wrong, and what His will is. Call it a feeling, a knowing, an intuition, or a green light on the inside, we all have a witness in our spirit when something is in question. You get a witness about certain people that tells you they are lying or that they are hiding something. You get a witness about certain opportunities and whether you should "go" or "not go."

This is not usually an audible voice, just a witness in our heart. It is a spiritual directive about what we should do or not do. Even people who do not know God have some ability to discern. But for the Christian, the Holy Spirit is inside to tell us what to do.

There are times when we miss it. We are human and make mistakes. We misunderstand what we feel and the witness we sense. But as we grow in the Lord and become more sensitive to the witness, it gets clearer, and we sense more clearly what to do.

It's like developing an ear for music. Most people hear only a small part of the sounds in a song. They listen to the words, and they hear one or two instruments. The fact is there are dozens of sounds in the production of music, and the trained ear picks them up. It hears bass, percussion, strings, and vocals. So it is with the witness of the Spirit: With practice and focus on your inner being, you learn to hear the witness of the Spirit.

Sometimes the directive of the witness may be contrary to what your reason tells you. Not that we are to turn off our brains, but there are times when God leads us beyond natural knowl-

edge. I recall a time when my congregation and I were faced with a decision about church facilities. It was a major decision, and several of the elders were nervous about it. After much prayer, discussion, and counsel from other leaders, it came down to decision time. All I had to go on was a witness of the Holy Spirit on what He wanted us to do. There were arguments for and against the project. There were also other options that seemed viable. In the end I had to decide, and I went with the witness of the Spirit, not any other rationale. Since the project has begun, I've seen more clearly why God led us the way He did and why the project will be such a great addition to our ministry campus.

Follow the witness in your spirit. Sometimes you can't explain it; you just know it. You may make mistakes, but you'll pick yourself up and go again. God wants to direct your life by the Spirit within you. Let Him do it.

6. What do mature Christians see in you?

You are not alone. God will bring to you friends and leaders who can help you on to destiny's course.

> *A man who isolates himself seeks his own desire;*
> *He rages against all wise judgment. (Prov. 18:1)*

Don't try to make every decision on your own. Use the gifts and talents of others. Although you cannot rely on them for any final decisions (you must be responsible for that), you can draw wisdom and insight from them. Remember—we are the body of Christ. No member of our body functions completely separately from the other members. Our eyes need the brain to do their job. Our hand needs the arm to do its job. We should not try to discern and fulfill our destiny alone.

One of the tragedies of our society is loneliness. With secularization came isolation, distrust, and loneliness. So many people have no one to pray with, to be honest and transparent with, or to seek counsel from. You may feel there's no one trustworthy with whom you can talk about your life and destiny. It's time to reach out, trust someone, and build some relationships.

But don't rely on one person to meet all your needs. Build relationships with several folks at your church (Yes, for some of you it's time to go back to church!) or wherever you know mature Christian people. It takes time, and some people won't "pan out." Some may let you down. But the pros of friendship outweigh the cons.

> *Where there is no counsel, the people fall;*
> *But in the multitude of counselors there is safety. (Prov. 11:14)*

You can't make all the right decisions on your own. Even when it comes to raising kids or handling money, we need input from others. But be sure you are seeking counsel from mature Christian people. Your dad or Uncle Bob may not be the best source of information.

> *Blessed is the man*
> *Who walks not in the counsel of the ungodly,*
> *Nor stands in the path of sinners,*
> *Nor sits in the seat of the scornful. (Ps. 1:1)*

When you walk with someone, you will eventually stand with them. So be careful with whom you associate.

> *He who walks with wise men will be wise,*
> *But the companion of fools will be destroyed. (Prov. 13:20)*

Take a good look at your closest friends. Whether you realize it or not, you are becoming like them, and they like you. If their marriages are bad, they may negatively impact yours. If they are struggling with financial problems, they may negatively affect your financial life. If they always struggle with their health, they may put doubts in your mind about your own health. Be careful whom you choose as your close friends; the companion of fools will be destroyed.

7. What career or ministry do you feel the peace of God about pursuing?

When we are on course with our God-given destiny, there is a peace that passes understanding in our life. Others may wonder how we can do what we are doing and have peace about it.

> *Be anxious for nothing, but in everything by prayer and supplication, with thanksgiving, let your requests be made known to God; and the peace of God, which surpasses all understanding, will guard your hearts and minds through Christ Jesus. (Phil. 4:6-7)*

This peace goes beyond the natural mind. It defies understanding or explanation. It is a supernatural part of knowing you are on course with God and with your destiny—knowing that before the foundation of the world, God established a destiny for you and that you are on the way to fulfilling it.

There have been several times throughout the history of Christian Faith Center when things were not easy. Financial needs, people problems, staff changes, and personal doubt are just a few of the things that have caused me some frustration. Nevertheless, after prayer, meditation, and discussion with friends, I always come back to that peace that surpasses understanding. I have a sense that the way has been prepared for me, and though the hill gets steep and long, I will make it. I will finish the course.

I'm convinced that many of those who suffer from heart attacks, ulcers, and headaches do not know this peace. They don't know or they doubt God's destiny for them, so they worry and wonder about decisions. They have no peace and soon lose control of their emotions, feelings, and health.

Paul told us that the peace of God would guard our hearts and minds. The use of the word "guard" implies a garrison or protective force that stops the destructive forces of fear, anxiety, and confusion. "God has not given us a spirit of fear, but of power and of love and of a sound mind" (2 Tim. 1:7).

When we walk in peace it is easier to love those who may try to use and abuse us. With the peace of God guarding our hearts and minds we can get better—not bitter—no matter what the challenge. The peace of God allows us to go home at night and

not let the cares of the day intrude on our time with our spouse and children. When problems arise, the peace of God keeps us from "freaking out" and getting off course. In His peace we just keep moving forward in destiny.

Isaiah 26:3 tells us, "You will keep him in perfect peace, whose mind is stayed on You, because he trusts in You." When we know our destiny, we trust God to lead us day by day and to help us reach our goals. We can be at perfect peace. Our mind will be clear and focused, and peace will rule our life. When we focus on the troubles, fears, and worries of life, we lose the peace of God.

Colossians 3:15 says:

> *And let the peace of God rule in your hearts, to which also you were called in one body; and be thankful.*

The Amplified Bible says to let the peace of God be the "umpire of your life." Let it call the balls and strikes. Let it say whether a decision is safe or out of the question. Let God's peace direct the game of life so you will stay in order and under control.

DESTINY KEY

LET THE PEACE OF GOD BE THE UMPIRE OF YOUR LIFE.

You can imagine what would happen if athletes were left to their own decisions on a playing field. The pitcher would never agree with the batter. Basketball players would kill each other, and the game would be chaos. Umpires and referees bring order and discipline to the game.

So it is in your life. As you find peace with God and man, you find a place of strength and order. Confusion is kept to a minimum and order is present in your heart and mind. Disagreement with yourself no longer drains your energy or restricts your grasp.

8. What thoughts, visions, or dreams are impossible to put out of your mind?

In Acts 2:17, we find that the Holy Spirit was giving visions and dreams to all flesh, young and old. They were full of ideas.

We can be too. We have the same Spirit. Most of the time when the Lord plants something in our spirit, it becomes a thought or an idea that just won't go away. "The spirit of a man is the lamp of the LORD, searching all the inner depths of his heart" (Prov. 20:27). God turns the light on inside us and we can't extinguish it.

Moses had thoughts of freeing his people for forty years before it was accomplished. From the time he was a child, Jeremiah had visions of ministering God's Word to his people. Often these thoughts and visions are the light of the Lord working in our spirit and signifying our destiny.

DESTINY KEY

EVERYTHING GOD WANTS TO DO IN YOUR LIFE WILL START AS A THOUGHT OR VISION.

As a young Christian, I began to think about what I could do to help others and make a difference in their lives. At that point, I was already on the course of destiny, but I didn't know much about what my destiny would look like. My dream of helping others stayed with me for years and grew into a vision of Christian Faith Center. What helped me see more fully my God-given destiny was the fact that I could not reject or escape my desire to help others. Finally I realized it was the will of the Lord for my life. What thoughts, visions, or ideas are going around inside you?

We often bury these things under a pile of doubt, fear, and rationalizations for why it could never work. But when we begin to move toward our destiny, all fear of failure goes away.

Those thoughts and visions and dreams that stay with you may indicate God's plan for your destiny.

9. To what can you give 100 percent of yourself for your whole life?

Whatever God planned for you will use all your gifts, talents, strengths, and emotions. He did not give you abilities only to ignore them in His destiny for you. First John 3:16 says that "we

also ought to lay down our lives for the brethren." God will ask us to give everything we have for the people we serve. Fulfilling one's destiny is not an easy, part-time job you can cruise through half asleep. You will be stretched to the limit. You will use everything within you, and you will have to dig deeply to finish your course (2 Tim. 4:7).

One of the greatest tragedies in our world today is the number of people who go to work every day but never use what is really in them. They drive down the freeway with their brain still asleep. They float through the day just trying to get by. They feel they are successful if they just keep a job. It's called "making a living" and it is a low level of life. Dogs make a living trying to be "man's best friend"; monkeys make a living finding bananas. But we have been given abundant life. We are called to live that life to the fullest, not to just make a living. We are to live the life that has been given to us by God from before the foundation of the world.

10. What do people want to gather around and help you accomplish?

The final question you should consider to discover your destiny is this: What do people want to help me do? This may apply more to those in leadership, but I think we can all use it.

After Paul had seen a vision of the Macedonian and had shared it with his ministry team, notice their response as recorded by Luke:

> *Now after he had seen the vision, immediately we sought to go to Macedonia, concluding that the Lord had called us to preach the gospel to them.* (Acts 16:10)

Paul had the vision, but all of those with him immediately picked it up and were willing to go with it. That happens when destiny is there. People sense it and get involved.

Churches, ministries, and businesses that are born of God attract people, and, like a magnet, get them involved with the vision. Departments in the church or in businesses that are destined to prosper attract the necessary people to make them succeed. When no one is interested and no one will get involved, it could be (though not always) that this is not a part of destiny.

Steps to Your Destiny

1. What is the deepest desire of your heart?
2. What stirs your passion?
3. What flows naturally out of you?
4. Where do you bring forth fruit or produce good results?
5. What is the witness of the Holy Spirit in your spirit?
6. What do mature Christians see in you?
7. What career or ministry do you feel the peace of God about pursuing?
8. What thoughts, visions, or dreams are impossible to put out of your mind?
9. To what can you give 100 percent of yourself for your whole life?
10. What do people want to gather around and help you accomplish?

4

Believing You Are Who God Says You Are

Genesis 1 recounts the story of the creation of man. God describes what people are all about, who they are, and the purpose of their creation. When we go back to this "Owner's Manual," we get the straight story.

In Genesis 1:26-28, God said:

> *"Let Us make man in Our image, according to Our likeness; let them have dominion over the fish of the sea, over the birds of the air, and over the cattle, over all the earth and over every creeping thing that creeps on the earth." So God created man in His own image; in the image of God He created him; male and female He created them. Then God blessed them, and God said to them, "Be fruitful and multiply; fill the earth and subdue it."*

"Then God saw everything that He had made, and indeed it was very good" (Gen. 1:31). God created us in His likeness and image, and He said we were not just good—but very good!

DESTINY KEY

BELIEVE WHAT GOD SAYS ABOUT YOU!

Through years of history, through various ideologies and philosophies, we have lost the revelation of who we are and what

we were created to be. We have gotten so far away from our foundations that some have decided men are accidents of evolution, just monkeys that shaved a little too close one day, just some kind of animal that evolved from nature accidentally. Freaks. Unexplained beings.

When individuals don't know their purpose and their creator, they live animalistic lives. They live far below their potential. And so we see the current condition of our society. People don't like themselves because they don't know who they are. And because they don't like themselves, they don't like anyone around them.

If you will get back to knowing who you are and what God says about you, if you will believe what God says more than what society says, more than what the government or a philosopher or a counselor says, then and only then will you rise to your full potential and experience your God-given destiny. *Believe what God says about you!* Then you will rise to the high level of life that is possible for you as a creation of God.

Some religions tell you that you're nothing but a worm or a dog. You're just dirt. They heap guilt and condemnation on you. But God says to you, "My child, lift up your head and come boldly unto the throne of grace where you will find mercy and help in your time of need." God crowns us with glory and honor.

Don't get me wrong. I know there's a place where we bow before the Lord. But it's time that we believe we are who God says we are: His children. It's time we carry ourselves with a sense of destiny and dignity. It's time we took our place as creatures who have been given dominion over the earth. We haven't known who we are, so we've lived far below our potential.

All Things Are Under Your Feet

God says to us, "Get out from under the economy. Get out from under the recession. Get out from under the fear and depression and discouragement of the world. Get out from under the circumstances and challenges and difficulties. Stand on top of them, for *all things are under your feet.*"

It's an amazing fact that how you think truly affects how you live. If you think, "I'm the victim of circumstances," then you often are. Similarly, if you think, "I've been created by God and all things are under my feet," then they often are.

Dead religion is so foolish. It says, "Love God and love your neighbor, but hate yourself because you're ungodly and unworthy."

And so we have this self-inflicted hatred of our own person. Then we try to love God and love our neighbor, and it just doesn't work. If we can grasp what God says to us—"You're My son. You're My daughter. You're created in My likeness, in My image. You're crowned with glory and honor. You can have dominion over this earth. All you have to do is love Me and love yourself and love your neighbor"—then we can believe in everyone around us.

Proverbs 23:7 tells us, "As he [man] thinks in his heart, so is he." Someone said to me, "Brother Treat, I just can't go for this 'as a man thinketh' stuff."

I said, "What do you mean? It's in the Bible."

He said, "I just don't think it works. If it's really true that you become whatever you think about, by the time I was seventeen years old, I'd have been either a girl or a Chevy!"

Forsake Those Limiting Thoughts

Let the wicked forsake his way,
And the unrighteous man his thoughts;
Let him return to the LORD,
And He will have mercy on him;
And to our God,
For He will abundantly pardon. (Isa. 55:7)

To return to the Lord is to forsake your thoughts. I wish God would give me the ability to empower you to forsake your thoughts. When I see people who have been Christians for years and their finances are still flatline—they're not growing, just maintaining year after year—I'm disturbed. When I see human beings created in the likeness and image of God, crowned with glory and honor and

given the power to have dominion, and yet they are satisfied with unrewarding jobs, mediocre marriages, or half-hearted prayer lives, it keeps me awake at night. You might call me intense, but I want to help people grow *from glory to glory*. It's not enough to say "amen" to a new revelation. We must forsake our thoughts and accept His thoughts.

> *"For My thoughts are not your thoughts,*
> *Nor are your ways My ways," says the* LORD.
> *"For as the heavens are higher than the earth,*
> *So are My ways higher than your ways,*
> *And My thoughts than your thoughts."* (Isa. 55:8-9)

When we get God's thoughts, we will get God's ways. As long as we hang on to our negative thoughts about ourselves and the world around us, we'll stay stuck in our ways. But when we forsake those thoughts and get God's thoughts, then we get God's ways.

DESTINY KEY

WHEN WE GET GOD'S THOUGHTS, WE WILL GET GOD'S WAYS.

The thoughts of the world are subtle. They never come marked in red, saying, "Warning! Warning! This is an ungodly thought!" They come disguised as insights or revelations. That's the way the enemy works.

A thought may come, and you'll begin to accept it. For example, you may be a businessperson with a young family. You're trying to build the business, but every day you hear about these new tax laws that are making things harder. The recession is hanging on and times are tough. It's hard, and it's tight, and you've got to really fight. They're closing down military bases. Businesses are closing all over the place. There's so much unemployment. This is a hard time. You hear it over and over.

Pretty soon you begin to believe it—subconsciously if not consciously. Eventually, you say to yourself, "This is a hard time, and it's tough out there. Making a profit is not easy." And you don't realize that your thoughts are contrary to God's thoughts, that your thoughts are lower than God's thoughts.

You've got to forsake them. He's the same God in the nineties as He was in the eighties and the seventies and the sixties. God is God! And He has the power to transcend economic conditions, to transcend all conditions. He told us so in His Word. Do you believe God or do you believe the news? *You have to choose.*

You might say, "But I don't have much education." All right, let's just take a poll of all the corporate heads of America and see how many don't have much education.

Or you might say, "But look at the color of my skin." Okay, let's just take a look around the world and see if there is anybody of your race who is growing and prospering.

You might say, "Brother Treat, do you know how old I am?" Let's see if we can find anybody your age who is growing and prospering. I mean spiritually, mentally, physically, and financially—in every way.

You might say, "But I'm overweight." Well, let's see if we can find anyone who is overweight yet doing well, growing, moving, and improving.

Think God's Thoughts About Yourself

What people have said about us isn't necessarily what God has said. People may tell us we're unworthy, but God has never said that. People may tell us we're lowlife, but God says we are created in His likeness and in His image. Sure, we've all behaved badly and displayed a negative attitude. But God never stops seeing us as valuable and precious, worthy to die for.

DESTINY KEY

GOD NEVER STOPS SEEING US AS VALUABLE AND PRECIOUS, WORTHY TO DIE FOR AND WORTHY TO LIVE FOR.

God says, "I know the thoughts that I think toward you . . . thoughts of peace and not of evil, to give you a future and a hope" (Jer. 29:11). God is thinking well of us. He's not looking to put us down. He wants to give us a future and a hope.

What are your thoughts about you? When you think about yourself, is it with the thoughts of God? Or with the thoughts that you picked up from this world? You'll have God's higher peace and His higher way of life when you have His higher thoughts.

Three Issues That Control Your Self-Image

There are three things that control the self-image of most people:

1. The Past

Most of our thoughts about ourselves in the present are based on things from our past. It could be past failures or successes, past comments, past teaching, or past examples. Things that were picked up in the past generally influence the way we are today.

I want you to look at a story with me in Genesis 19. You know the story about Sodom and Gomorrah. These ancient cities were wicked places. Homosexuality was rampant, and people were locked into their evil ways.

God said, "I'm going to judge and destroy this place." But first He had to get Lot and his family out safely. So the angels came and took Lot and his wife and two daughters and said, "Get out of town, and don't look back!"

As they were escaping to the mountains,

> *The LORD rained brimstone and fire on Sodom and Gomorrah, from the LORD out of the heavens. So He overthrew those cities . . . all the inhabitants of the cities, and what grew on the ground. But his [Lot's] wife looked back behind him, and she became a pillar of salt. (Gen. 19:24-26)*

In a spiritual sense, I believe there are many Christians who continually look back, and they have become pillars of salt. They're not moving; they're not growing; they're not increasing or improving. They're just looking back.

Someone once said to me, "Remember when we used to have church in the gymnasium? Oh, man, that was so special. I remem-

ber the services that we had back there. I wish we could have that kind of praise and worship today."

Now, I have a tape of that service back in the gym. You don't want to hear it. It was bad, even on a good day. That's what we had then. We were excited, and it was good at that time. But to go back would be to regress.

My children had something on television one day, and I sat down and watched it with them. I realized it was an original *Superman*. I wish I hadn't seen that program, because I saw the original *Superman* when I was eight, and back then he was cool. At that time he looked like the real Superman, and he did things that a real Superman was supposed to do. He solved crimes and saved Metropolis time after time. As I watched that program thirty years later, I thought it was corny—bad acting, bad plot, bad everything! I hate it when reality ruins my memory. When we remember the good old days, we are usually exercising selective memory. Sometimes that keeps us from moving ahead.

Of course, we also selectively recall the negative, when we were abused, raped, or molested, when our dad said, "You're nobody, and you're never going to amount to a hill of beans." Or "If your head weren't screwed on, you'd lose it too."

We look back and remember those thoughts, those incidents, those situations, and we relive that hurt. We forget that we're not twelve or fourteen anymore. We just keep carrying those things around as if they were real right now. And looking back, we're paralyzed. We become pillars of salt, spiritually speaking. It keeps us from going on to the destiny that God has for us.

Paul said in Philippians 3:13-14:

> *One thing I do, forgetting those things which are behind and reaching forward to those things which are ahead, I press toward the goal for the prize of the upward call of God in Christ Jesus.*

You've got to forget the past. You've got to leave it, the good stuff and the bad. It's past. It's history. Let it go! Stop looking back! It will weigh you down and keep you from being all that you can be.

2. Lack of Vision

Many of us are controlled by the future. You say, "That sounds strange." But it's true. Where there is no vision, people scatter, like sheep without a shepherd. Lack of vision brings fear, worry, doubt, and confusion into people's lives. They look ahead and say, "What are we going to do?"

Fear of the future is what causes people to say, "Please give me a job and health insurance. Please take care of me. Just promise me that everything is going to be okay."

The Antichrist will use this mind-set to his advantage when he sets up his kingdom. He will be a great world leader who promises peace and health care. He'll say, "I'll take care of you." People are going to be so fearful that they will buy into it.

God has put tremendous ability, creative power, and potential in you. But if you look to the future with fear and trepidation, your potential and creative power are stifled.

Ray Kroc was past fifty, selling milk-shake blenders, and doing pretty well. Then he got a vision of McDonald's hamburgers around the country. In his book, Grinding It Out, Kroc says, "Everybody believed that you couldn't prosper in those days because of the tax situation, the economy, the recession. It was too hard to get ahead. There was no more opportunity in America." He was fifty-four when he started McDonald's, and it was 1977 when he wrote his book. They were saying the same thing back when Ray started that they're saying today.

DESTINY KEY

GOD HAS PUT TREMENDOUS ABILITY, CREATIVE POWER, AND POTENTIAL IN YOU.

Another book I picked up recently was written in the forties, and you know what? It said the same thing! "Can't get ahead. It's too hard. The government . . . taxes . . . recession." I saw the same line in another book. This one was published in the 1800s! Every generation is the same. There are always those who believe you can and those who believe you can't. You must decide which you are going to be.

Ray Kroc decided he would start McDonald's. We know the story from there. We've all benefited from his vision. I have more McDonald's toys in my house than anyone! Kroc wasn't afraid of the future. He didn't say it was negative or bleak. He didn't mutter, "Woe is me, what am I going to do?" He said, "Let's go get 'em!"

Most of you are going to live through this year. What are you going to do with yourself? Why don't you decide right now that you won't let laziness edge out your prayer time, that you'll commit to growing in God through prayer and through studying His Word. Get a vision like Kroc did. Decide right now how much money you're going to make. Decide to do a little bit better than make a living. Decide how much you're going to weigh at the end of the year. You're going to weigh something, so why don't you decide today how much that's going to be. Get a vision! This could be your greatest year!

"But I've tried before . . ."

There's your past speaking. Are you going to let it control your future?

"But I'm afraid . . ."

Don't let the future be negative. Don't let it be bleak. Get a vision of a bright future!

3. Comparisons

You are a unique individual. You are created in God's likeness and image. You are unlike anyone else, and you cannot be compared.

> *For we dare not class ourselves or compare ourselves with those who commend themselves. But they, measuring themselves by themselves, and comparing themselves among themselves, are not wise.* (2 Cor. 10:12)

God says, "Don't try to be like someone else. I like you the way you are." You're a good you, while at best a mediocre somebody else.

When you compare yourself with other people, one of two things happens. You put others down to lift yourself up. "I make more money." "My wife's prettier." "My husband is more hand-

some." "I know more Bible verses." "I've led more people to Christ." "I have a better job."

The second option is to put yourself down by looking at others, and saying, "I wish I were as good as they are," or " I wish I had a job like they have," or "I wish I had a family like they have," or "I wish I had a house like they have." When you compare yourself with others, you're acting unwisely.

What good would it do for us to compare professional basketball player Shawn Kemp with professional football player Joe Montana? It's an irrelevant comparison. It's a waste of time. It's erroneous. Shawn Kemp is a great athlete. Joe Montana is a great athlete. Comparing the two would be irrelevant and immaterial because there is no comparison.

Joe wouldn't last for one quarter on the floor of an NBA game. Every time he tried to take a shot, somebody would stuff the ball down his throat. And, of course, Shawn Kemp out there on the football field, the first hit—WHAM—he's history. He's out for the season. But we don't need to compare them because each has his own game. One can't be compared to the other.

Now, God predestined you before the foundation of the world, and God gave you a game. Your game doesn't compare to mine or to anybody else's. What you need to win at your game doesn't compare to what I need to win at my game. What you do to be successful in your life doesn't compare with what others do to be successful in their lives.

Someone said to me, "Pastor Treat, I could never do what you do." I answered him, "You don't need to! God hasn't called you to do what He's called me to do."

We each have our own game of life, and we can all be stars. God gives each of us the gifts and the talents and the abilities to be a superstar in our own game. We can all be the best. We can all be in the all-star game, because in your game, you're the best. God made you that way. God gifted you and enabled you to be victorious. If you start messing with my area of destiny, you're going to fail. If Shawn gets on the football field, it's over. If Joe gets on the basketball court, it's over. If we compare ourselves with one other and start trying to be like one other and live out someone else's destiny, we're going to fail. But if we will just be

who God created us to be and do what God created us to do and not compare ourselves, we'll win!

As a pastor, I would meet with the other pastors in the ministerial meetings, and we would all compare:

"How many people did you have in church Sunday?"

"How much money did you get in the offerings on Sunday?"

"How many folks responded to the altar call on Sunday?"

"How many buildings do you have? How much square footage?"

Let me add that it's not always bad to compare yourself to others. Sometimes it can be healthy, although we rarely practice this positive form of comparison. It is good to look at someone else and be inspired by his or her prayer life and say, "I want to learn to pray like he does"; or to see the time a father spends with his children and think, "I need to be an attentive father like him"; or to read about a great man or woman of God and say, "I want to live a life for God with a passion like hers." These are healthy comparisons.

But the fact is that we do much less of the above and a lot more of the trivial and destructive sort of comparing: Somebody is thinner than you are. Somebody has prettier hair than you have. Somebody has bigger muscles. Somebody has something you wish you had. Such comparing will never bring you to a place of feeling good about yourself. But that's how most of us live. This applies on all levels. We compare our talents to theirs. We compare our friends to theirs. We compare our children to theirs. We compare our car to their car. We compare our house to their house. We compare what we do to what they do. We compare the size of our office door to the other doors, the size of our office to the other offices, the size of our desk to the other desks.

"How big is your window?"

"Well, I have a view of the water."

Even around our church, when we move people from one desk to another, we have a crisis.

"What's wrong?"

"Well, the other office had a window."

Or "My other office had two shelves; this one has only one shelf."

What's going on? Self-esteem controlled by comparison. God says it isn't wise to compare ourselves.

Loving Your Neighbor as Yourself

Jesus was talking with the Pharisees when one of them asked Him a question.

> *"Teacher, which is the great commandment in the law?" Jesus said to him, "'You shall love the* LORD *your God with all your heart, with all your soul, and with all your mind.' This is the first and great commandment. And the second is like it: 'You shall love your neighbor as yourself.'"* (Matt. 22:36-39)

Now notice they asked for one great commandment, but Christ gave them two. You cannot do one of these without doing the other. The two go together, hand in hand. Love God and love your neighbor as yourself. Unless we obey both commandments, we will not be able to live the life that God planned for us.

God said, "First of all, you've got to love God with all your heart. Second, you must love your neighbor as yourself." On those two commandments hang all the Law and the Prophets. All sixty-six books of the Bible, everything from Genesis to Revelation, hangs on those two commandments: (1) love God, and (2) love your neighbor as yourself.

DESTINY KEY

WHEN YOU BELIEVE IN YOURSELF, YOU BEGIN TO BELIEVE IN THE PEOPLE AROUND YOU.

I remember struggling as a young Christian and asking myself how I was going to make it. How would I live the Christian life and have any kind of success in life? I was praying one day and sensed the Holy Spirit bringing this verse to my mind. The Holy Spirit said to me, "That's the problem with you. You love your neighbor as yourself." And I said, "Well, Lord, am I not supposed to do that?" He said to me, "Yes, but you hate yourself."

When you love yourself, you begin to love the people around you. You desire to bless them, help them, lift them, enable them, and empower them. But when you feel bad about yourself, you feel jealous, competitive, angry, separated, and isolated.

Society as a whole illustrates this principle. Knowingly or unknowingly we treat everyone around us as we treat ourselves. If we can love God and love ourselves, we'll have no problem loving our neighbors.

The kid in a gang is not going to respond to a gun law. I'm not saying we shouldn't have gun laws. I'm just saying that just because the law says he shouldn't have that gun, doesn't mean that he's going to say, "Oh, okay," and get rid of it. He needs to find out who God is and who he is. If we could ever get the greatest law into his mind and his heart—the law of God—if we could ever get him to see that he is a creation of God—with destiny, with dignity, with glory, with honor—then he would begin to love himself and he wouldn't need the gun anymore. He's not going to want the drugs or alcohol anymore. When you love yourself, you begin to love those around you. Then you will love your neighbor as you love yourself.

The husband who is frustrated and bitter, who hates his wife, doesn't need a new wife. He needs to love himself. Then he can love his wife as he loves himself. He needs to find out who he is in God's eyes.

A Higher Life

As a whole, Christians live far below the level of what the Word says about them. My mission as a pastor is to lead people to a higher life so they will be all God created them to be. I want to live life to the fullest and be all that He says I am. I want to fulfill my destiny.

The fact that I am a shepherd does not mean that *I've got it together*. When the shepherd leads the sheep, they stay together, and together they go to the green pastures. I'm not there yet. But I'm on my way, and I want to help you be on your way too. So together our purpose is to find out who we are and to become what God created us to be.

We all have a great destiny. Great potential has been placed in each of us by God. Let's go for it. Let's maximize it. Let's experience it. God says, "You're created in My likeness, in My image." He says, "You're crowned with glory and honor. You have dominion, and all things are under your feet."

You may say, "Well, Brother Treat, under the circumstances I'm currently facing, I just don't think I can have a consistent daily time with God"; or "I just don't think I can go to my boss and ask for the raise I deserve"; or "I just don't think I can be more patient with my spouse." What? What are you doing under there? Whose foot are you under? God said all things are under *your* feet.

Most of us function from a perspective of what parents, schools, government, or religion says or has said about us more than we focus on what God has said about us. We live at a lower level of life because of how we think about ourselves. We blame government for our economic situation; we blame society for our social situation; we blame our spouse for our marital situation. We blame something or someone for the conditions of our life. But I'm saying to you that *your life in many ways is a manifestation of what you think about yourself,* not what others have said or done.

As a young girl, my wife, Wendy, struggled with her reading and writing. A frustrated teacher said to her, "You'll never be a good writer. You'll never be good at reading, and you will never be a good communicator." Wendy carried the pain of that prediction for years. The words of that teacher caused her to be embarrassed about her writing.

As freshmen in Bible school, Wendy and I were writing papers for our assignments. After they were graded by the teacher, the papers were put into a particular box where we picked them up. Being a good boyfriend, I went to the box and picked up Wendy's paper along with mine. I sat down in the library and read Wendy's paper. When I was halfway through, she came into the library and walked over to me. When she saw me reading her paper, she shrieked, grabbed the paper out of my hand, and ran out of the library. I sat there saying, "What?!"—not knowing that the negative words of her teacher had so programmed Wendy's mind (she believed them) that she was embarrassed. She didn't want me to know how "bad" her writing was. She actually

thought that because I wanted to be a pastor, I would no longer want to be with her because she couldn't write or communicate. It didn't matter that she got 100 percent on the paper. It didn't matter that she got A's in school. It didn't matter that those negative statements weren't true. Her mind had absorbed the criticism of a teacher—a respected person—and she was living by those criticisms every day.

Finally we talked about it, and she began to realize who she really was. Today she is one of the preeminent woman ministers in this nation. I'd like to look up that old teacher and ask her how many books she's written, how many nations she's preached in, how many thousands of people she's spoken to. If you knew where Wendy started, you would see what the process of learning to believe in herself has done.

Release That Steel Trap!

Several people came to me not long ago and told me that Rick Godwin, a pastor friend of mine in San Antonio, Texas, had mentioned me on TV. He'd said, "You know, Casey Treat has a mind like a steel trap." As I thought about it, I realized that everyone has a mind like a steel trap. We clamp down on thoughts, words, and attitudes, and we hold them for years.

Your father might have said, "I'm sick and tired of you bugging me. Get out of my hair." And your mind snapped down on that thought and said, "I'm not loved." A relative or a person abused you, used you, molested you, and your mind grabbed that feeling, that fear, that anxiety and has held it even until now. It could be ten years, twenty years, forty years later, but your mind is still holding that emotion.

You failed at some sport and somebody said, "You'll never be athletic." BAM! The trap snapped down on that thought, and you hang on to it even until today.

It's not easy to escape a trap. It's not easy to change a thought. You have to grab hold of both sides and pull. That's what ministers are trying to do when we preach about renewing the mind. We're trying to get you to forcefully pull back the jaws of that steel trap, that brain of yours, and release those old thoughts,

those old beliefs that you would never prosper physically, spiritually, or emotionally. They may be thoughts that say you will never be healthy and strong, or that you will never have the kind of marriage you really desire, or that you'll never control your weight.

Here's the great news. You can open the trap! You can release those thoughts! Do it! You can replace them with what God says about you in His Word, and you can be all that God says you are.

Pray this with care:

Father, help me to be all that You created me to be. Help me to see myself through Your eyes. Help me to throw off the negativity of the past—the judgments, the criticisms, and limitations imposed on me by people, religion, and society. Oh God, help me rise to that higher level of life.

Steps to Your Destiny

1. What does God say about you? (Only as you know this will you reach full potential and fulfill your destiny.)

2. Have others bombarded you with negative thoughts about yourself? Which thoughts should you release and replace with God's thoughts about you?

3. Because of your worldview, how do you limit yourself and your potential?

4. Read and apply the following verses to yourself to renew your self-image.

   Genesis 1:26-28
   Psalm 8
   Matthew 6:24-34
   Matthew 12:33-35
   Philippians 4:13, 19
   Ephesians 2:10
   1 John 5:1-4
   2 Corinthians 5:17-21

5

Moving from Insecurity to Confidence

"God said, 'Let Us make man in Our image, according to Our likeness" (Gen. 1:26). God made you! *You're not an evolutionary freak.* You're a creation of God, made in His image! Many scientists today laugh at the theory of evolution. They know it's a theory. The idea is far-fetched, and there is no evidence to endorse it. The more scientists learn, the more their discoveries support the theory that a sovereign power created this world, including you and me. They may not call that power "God" as of yet, because God would have to get into their test tubes and show them a sign. But one day they will discover that it's true.

You may say to me, "You don't understand. I was an accident. My parents didn't want kids." Or "I was an accident. I don't even know who my father was." Or "My mother gave me up for adoption."

Your mother or father may not have known your purpose or why you were created. But God did. God transcends moms and dads, one-night stands, adoptions, and everything else. God says, "I created you in My likeness and in My image. And I created you with a destiny." That destiny includes having dominion, ruling, and reigning. It means having an abundant life, not just a "barely get by" life. To know your destiny, you need to break away from your insecurity into a life of confidence.

Studies have proven that our thinking controls our behavior. Classroom experiments demonstrate that when a teacher is told the students in his or her classroom are slower than the other students in the school, he or she instructs on a lower level. Soon those students begin to function at a lower level, regardless of their intelligence or capabilities.

DESTINY KEY

AS A MAN THINKS, SO IS HE.

Conversely, when a teacher is told that a particular group (the same group of students) is above average, the teacher enters that classroom with a different mind-set and begins to teach to that higher level. She or he expects more from every child. Sure enough, over a period of time those students rise to that higher level and begin to perform at an above-average level.

If your mom or dad told you that you're worthless, you're going to live that way until that thought pattern is broken.

If somebody told you that you were just average, that you will have an average life and an average job, live in an average home and drive an average car, wear average clothes and have average looks—you're likely going to live on an average level until that thought pattern is broken. *As a man thinks, and as a woman thinks, so is he and so is she.*

What you think about yourself has an extremely strong influence in terms of the controlling factors of your life. What you think you can do, what you think you can be, what you believe about your life, has more control over you than the president or our society or the economy ever will. It can hamper or help you as you travel the road to discovering your destiny.

Sometimes we feel as though our problems make us different from everyone else, and that's why we can't go any further. Every person feels like there are special reasons why they are limited or stuck in their present lifestyle.

That is not meant to be a condemnation or a message that you aren't doing enough or working hard enough. That's not the point. The point is there are opportunities for all of us to experience more of God's will in our lives and our walks with Him. There's the privilege of abundant life that none of us have fully realized.

Many of the heroes in the Bible started just like you and me. Most were lowly, insecure, hurt, or frustrated. But they all had something in common: They were searching for their God-given destiny. And to the extent that they believed in themselves and their God, not giving in to negative thoughts, they all discovered and fulfilled their destinies. We assume that biblical figures were "super spiritual." But many struggled with the same human weaknesses we do. Some had low self-esteem. Some felt negative about themselves. Some came from dysfunctional families. Some were born in poverty. Like us, they were bound by insecurities and fears and anxieties. But they heard God and believed what He said about them. As a result, they became people of destiny.

Joseph

Let's look at the life of Joseph. He was the eleventh child in a family of twelve boys, so he had ten older brothers and one younger brother. He also had one sister. His father liked Joseph better than any of the other boys, and he bought Joseph things that he wouldn't buy the other children. He gave Joseph a coat of many colors, which none of the other boys had. Think about this family—four wives, thirteen children, and a dad who played favorites.

> *But when his brothers saw that their father loved him [Joseph] more than all his brothers, they hated him and could not speak peaceably to him. (Gen. 37:4)*

So Joseph's family was full of strife and hatred and competition. Joseph was on the receiving end of the emotional trauma of these circumstances.

A Dysfunctional Home

This sure sounds like a dysfunctional home. Joseph's siblings couldn't speak to him without anger and hatred. Here was a young man who really had a difficult childhood.

Genesis 37:5 says, "Now Joseph dreamed a dream, and he told it to his brothers." I believe his telling his brothers his dream

reveals his low self-image. It's as if he had to say, "Hey, guys, I'm cooler than you. I had a dream." As a result:

> *They hated him even more. So he said to them, "Please hear this dream which I have dreamed: There we were, binding sheaves in the field. Then behold, my sheaf arose and also stood upright; and indeed your sheaves stood all around and bowed down to my sheaf." (Gen. 37:5-7)*

Whoa! This was really going to improve family relationships! Then Joseph shared another dream with his brothers:

> *"Look, I have dreamed another dream. And this time, the sun, the moon, and the eleven stars bowed down to me." So he told it to his father and his brothers; and his father rebuked him and said to him, "What is this dream that you have dreamed? Shall your mother and I and your brothers indeed come to bow down to the earth before you?" (Gen. 37:9-10)*

Do you see the circumstances? This family was not harmonious, to say the least.

Betrayed by His Brothers

Joseph went out some time later to see his brothers in the field and to take them some food as they were caring for the sheep. He wore his coat of many colors. Unknown to Joseph, trouble lay ahead.

> *When they saw him afar off, even before he came near them, they conspired against him to kill him. Then they said to one another, "Look, this dreamer is coming!" (Gen. 37:18-19)*

Some of you were raised in families where there was a lot of pain and strife. And you've said, "I can't have an abundant life, a fulfilling destiny, because of the way I was raised."

But look at Joseph! He didn't come from a happy home. He didn't have a good relationship with his siblings. His family was a dysfunctional mess, and the rivalry was so bad his brothers were about to kill him.

> *"Come therefore, let us now kill him and cast him into some pit; and we shall say, 'Some wild beast has devoured him.' We shall see what will become of his dreams!" But Reuben heard it, and he delivered him out of their hands, and said, "Let us not kill him." (Gen. 37:20-21)*

Finally, in a last-minute ploy to save his brother's life, Judah said, "Don't kill him! Sell him!" So they sold Joseph into slavery under the Egyptians.

Set Up by a Seductress

Potiphar, who was an Egyptian official, took Joseph into his home as a servant, which presented Joseph with a choice. What would he do with his life? Would he be depressed and angry? Or would he trust God for his destiny? He began to serve Potiphar with his whole heart.

Soon Potiphar put him in charge of the other servants, and Joseph began managing the entire household. God was blessing him. But then Potiphar's wife began to notice the attractive young servant. She tried to seduce him. Joseph said, "I'm not going to lower myself to fornication or adultery. I have a God-given destiny." He resisted Potiphar's wife and ran from her, but she grabbed his coat as he was leaving. Then she lied about Joseph, and he was thrown into prison.

Back to the Pit

Joseph had to make another choice. What was he going to do? He hadn't just lost his job; he had been thrown in jail. He hadn't just lost his family; he had been sold into slavery. Some people living today, when treated like Joseph, might conclude: "I'm in jail. I'll become a drug user. That will make life easier." Or, "I'll live on Valium. I'll just take tranquilizers every day, and my life will be tolerable."

What would you do? Back in the pit, Joseph said to himself, "I'm going to run this prison. I'll become the warden." Joseph's vision always rose to the highest possible place wherever he was. Like Paul, who kept getting up when he was beaten and thrown outside the city gates, Joseph had a sense of destiny. When he

was with his family, he said, "You are all going to bow down to me." When he was with Potiphar he said, "I'm going to manage this house." When he was in jail he said, "I'm going to run this jail."

First Joseph was a trustee, but soon the prison keeper put him in charge of all the prisoners. Then a couple of staff members from Pharaoh's house were sent to jail: a butler and a baker. There they had upsetting dreams, which Joseph interpreted. The baker eventually was executed, but the butler was released and went back to work for Pharaoh.

From the Pit to the Palace

Before the butler left the jail, Joseph said to him, "When you go back to Pharaoh's house, remember me." But the butler forgot about Joseph, who lingered in jail two more years. Then Pharaoh had a troubling dream and said, "Who can interpret my dream?"

And the butler said, "I remember this guy back in prison. He interpreted my dream, and it came to pass. I bet he could interpret your dream, Pharaoh." So Pharaoh said, "Bring him up here." Joseph shaved and dressed, then he went before the pharaoh.

When Pharaoh told Joseph his dream, Joseph not only interpreted the dream but told him how to deal with the circumstances that were to come. He had a plan that would make the pharaoh successful and save the country. The pharaoh saw that there was something about Joseph—that he had discernment and wisdom that no other staff member in his court had. Pharaoh took his ring and put it on Joseph's hand and clothed him in fine clothes. He made him the head of the whole nation of Egypt. Other than Pharaoh, there was none higher than this Israelite.

Joseph accepted the position, the ring, and the robe and said, "Doesn't a chariot come with this position?"

"Oh, yes. You'll have the chariot right behind Pharaoh."

And, in the span of one day, Joseph began to run the whole nation of Egypt—he'd gone from the pit to the palace. Not by being bitter, angry, or vengeful. Not by talking about his dysfunctional family. Not by talking about his brothers, who hated him and sold him into slavery. But by trusting the Lord and

serving others. He took his place and fulfilled his dreams—his God-given destiny. The dream never died, even after all that he had gone through.

It doesn't matter what's happened to you or what you've done. God never stopped loving you, and He has planned a wonderful destiny for you. If you remember what the Father says about your life, who He says you are, what He says you can do—if you keep that God-given dream—you'll rise to your place in destiny. You can't keep dreamers in the pit. They rise from the pit to the palace, and nothing can stop them.

> ***DESTINY KEY***
>
> IF YOU HAVE A GOD-GIVEN DREAM, IF YOU KEEP AND NURTURE THAT DREAM, YOU CAN RISE TO THAT PLACE OF DESTINY.

Moses

In Exodus 3, we learn that Moses had been born in Egypt sometime after Joseph died. Because Pharaoh had ordered the death of all the male Hebrew infants, Moses' mother placed him in a tiny raft and floated him down the river, where he was found by Pharaoh's daughter.

From Pharaoh's Palace to the Desert

Pharaoh's daughter took Moses into the palace, and he was raised as her son. He had the best education in the highest culture of the then-known world. Some say he became a leader in Pharaoh's army. For forty years Moses lived in the lap of luxury. Then he decided he would make some changes and do something about the bondage of his own people, the Hebrews. (I believe at this point Moses had an inkling of what his destiny was, but he couldn't see it clearly.) He killed an Egyptian who was beating a Hebrew and then ran out of town. He went to the back side of the desert, where he hid in isolation and rejection. He began to herd sheep for an old shepherd and eventually married the shepherd's daughter.

Someone has said that Moses spent the first forty years of his life believing he was *somebody*. He spent the next forty years of his life finding out he was *nobody*. But then God came to him and he spent the last forty years of his life finding out that with God he was somebody.

Disheartened, Confused, and Lonely

In Exodus 3:2-6, the Lord came to Moses as he tended his father-in-law's flock.

> *And the Angel of the LORD appeared to him in a flame of fire from the midst of a bush. So he looked, and behold, the bush was burning with fire, but the bush was not consumed. Then Moses said, "I will now turn aside and see this great sight, why the bush does not burn." So when the LORD saw that he turned aside to look, God called to him from the midst of the bush and said, "Moses, Moses!" And he said, "Here I am." Then He said, "Do not draw near this place. Take your sandals off your feet, for the place where you stand is holy ground." Moreover He said, "I am the God of your father—the God of Abraham, the God of Isaac, and the God of Jacob." And Moses hid his face, for he was afraid to look upon God.*

Then the Lord told Moses that Moses was going to go back to Egypt and deliver the people of Israel. What was Moses' response?

> *"Who am I that I should go to Pharaoh, and that I should bring the children of Israel out of Egypt?" (Ex. 3:11)*

Talking Back to a Burning Bush

"Lord, You don't understand," Moses said. "I'm a nobody. I can't do it. I'm a failure. I tried forty years ago to do something, and it didn't work. I gave up. I've just been taking care of a few sheep all these years. Who am I to take on such an important job?"

The Lord said, "Don't worry. I'll be with you."

Eventually, Moses successfully led the Israelites out of Egypt. Yet where did Moses start? Feeling bad about himself, feeling inadequate, talking back to a burning bush, saying, "I can't."

When you feel inadequate, you get creative about why something won't work. You have a supernatural ability to convince yourself that things won't turn out well. Moses said, "God, what if they ask me Your name?"

God said to Moses, "You tell them that I am Yahweh, the God that is. I am your healer. I am your provider. I am your peace. I am your sanctifier. I am your righteousness. I am your strength."

> *Then Moses answered and said, "But suppose they will not believe me or listen to my voice; suppose they say, 'The LORD has not appeared to you.'" So the LORD said to him, "What is that in your hand?" He said, "A rod." And He said, "Cast it on the ground." So he cast it on the ground, and it became a serpent; and Moses fled from it. Then the LORD said to Moses, "Reach out your hand and take it by the tail" (and he reached out his hand and caught it, and it became a rod in his hand), . . . Furthermore the LORD said to him, "Now put your hand in your bosom." And he put his hand in his bosom, and when he took it out, behold, his hand was leprous, like snow. And He said, "Put your hand in your bosom again." So he put his hand in his bosom again, and drew it out of his bosom, and behold, it was restored like his other flesh. (Ex. 4:1-4, 6-7)*

Then God said to Moses, "Do you get the message?" Moses answered him in verse 10, "O my Lord, I am not eloquent." God must have wanted to say, "With rods turning into snakes and leprosy healed and bushes burning, who cares if you can talk! Mime your message!"

You see, when you feel inadequate, you create absurd reasons why you can't change.

"Lord, I don't have enough education."

"Lord, I've got no skills."

"Lord, I'm too young."

Who Made Your Mouth?

Moses' excuse was, "Lord, I can't talk."

> *"O my Lord, I am not eloquent, neither before nor since You have spoken to Your servant; but I am slow of speech and slow of tongue." (Ex. 4:10)*

Low self-esteem is powerful. Negative self-image is strong. But if we don't break it and get a new image—God's image—we'll never be what God created us to be.

In exasperation, God asked Moses, "Who made your mouth?" And Moses said, "Y-y-y-y-you did." And God said, "Then I'll make it work." And Moses said, "B-b-b-but, Lord."

Finally God sent Aaron to help Moses, and they started through a series of events to lead Israel out of Egypt.

Face to Face with God

Now how did Moses' story end? In the end of his life, he fulfilled his destiny. He was the mightiest man on the face of the earth. He stepped into the glory of God and talked to God face to face as no other man ever had before him or ever did after him. He was on the mount of God. He saw God while he sat in the cleft of the rock. He was in the Holy of Holies as the tabernacle was built, and he saw the shekinah glory. At one-hundred-twenty years old, his back was not weak and his eyes were not dim. He went to the top of Mount Nebo and stepped into the presence of God.

We still look at Moses as one of the greatest men of the Bible. But where did he begin? He couldn't talk. He was nervous. He had a low self-image. He had excuses for why he could never take the new position, why he could never fulfill his destiny. He was rationalizing and arguing with God. Why? He was stuck in a bad self-image.

You and I are no different from Moses. We have the same feelings, the same fears, the same thoughts. But if we'll do what Moses did, believe what God said and act on that belief, we'll rise above those things and begin to lead that company or that family or that student organization. We can have that abundant life. We can be whatever God has called us to be and do what God has called us to do. We can be people of destiny.

The Nation of Israel

When Israel was in the wilderness, Moses sent twelve spies into the promised land to check things out. When they came back, they said to Moses in Numbers 13:27, "We went to the land where you sent us. It truly flows with milk and honey."

> ***DESTINY KEY***
>
> WHEN YOU FEEL BAD ABOUT YOURSELF, YOU CREATE REASONS WHY YOU CAN'T CHANGE.

The land was great. It was good. It was beautiful. But they said, "The people who dwell in the land are strong; the cities are fortified and very large" (Num. 13:28).

Who does this sound like? It sounds like many of us. We say, "It's a great country, but there is a recession. The economy is down. I can't find a job. It's hard out there. There are problems—social problems, economic problems, family problems. We can't succeed."

> *"We are not able to go up against the people, for they are stronger than we."(Num. 13:31)*

How Do You See Yourself?

Notice that they didn't say, "God is not able." They said, "We are not able." They knew what God could do. They had seen His miracles in Egypt. God could defeat Egypt. He could overcome any old Canaanite. He could crush a Hittite, a Jebusite, or an Amorite. They knew what God could do, but they doubted themselves. They had that low self-image, that slavery mentality.

> *And they gave the children of Israel a bad report of the land which they had spied out, saying, "The land through which we have gone as spies is a land that devours its inhabitants, and all the people whom we saw in it are men of great stature. There we saw the giants (the descendants of Anak came from the giants); and we were like grasshoppers in our own sight." (Num. 13:32-33)*

There's the key! They said: "We were like grasshoppers in *our own* sight."

> ***DESTINY KEY***
>
> WHEN YOU BELIEVE YOU ARE WHO GOD SAYS YOU ARE, YOU WILL BE WHO GOD SAYS YOU CAN BE, YOU WILL HAVE WHAT GOD SAYS YOU CAN HAVE, AND YOU WILL DO WHAT GOD SAYS YOU CAN DO. YOU WILL FULFILL YOUR DESTINY.

How are you in your own sight? You may say, "Well, I'm making a living." That's too bad. What a shame.

"I'm getting by." Bummer. I'm sorry to hear that.

"Well, you know, I'm average." And here I thought you were a creation of God! I thought you were made in His likeness, in His image, able to do all things through Christ!

How are you in your own sight? "We were like grasshoppers in our own sight, *and so we were in their sight*" (Num. 13:33). Always remember: How you see yourself is how everybody else will see you.

Gideon

The book of Judges tells us about a man named Gideon who was in bad shape. He was poor. His country, Israel, had been taken over by the Midianites. The last thing he was after was his God-given destiny. All that was on Gideon's mind was how he would get his next meal. So Gideon hid in a wine press, trying to get enough wheat together to make a loaf of bread for the day.

Just Trying to Make a Living

It was there in the wine press that an angel came to him:

> *And the Angel of the* LORD *appeared to him, and said to him, "The* LORD *is with you, you mighty man of valor!" (Judg. 6:12)*

Now think about this. Here was a guy hiding in a wine press, trying to hoard enough threshed wheat for a loaf of bread, fearing the enemies all around him—a scared little wimp. Do you get the picture? And what did the angel of the Lord say to him?

"Whew, you're in bad shape, bud." Nope.

"Well, friend, life's got you down, huh?" Nope.

"Oh, boy, these *are* hard times, aren't they?" No!

The angel said, "The LORD is with you, you mighty man of valor!"

Gideon began to argue with the angel the same way Moses argued with God. Gideon said, "Lord, if You're with me, why am I in these circumstances?"

Similarly, you might say, "If God wants people to be healed, why didn't my spouse get healed?" Or "If God wants to bless my life, why do I have this lousy job?"

And the Lord said to Gideon, "Go in this might of yours, and you shall save Israel" (Judg. 6:14).

Gideon was just trying to make a loaf of bread. He wasn't even close to thinking about saving Israel. That's you and me. We're just trying to get to work on time. And God is saying to us, "I have so much more for your life. You can rise to greatness. What a destiny I have for you!"

But you say, "We're just trying to pay the rent and balance the checkbook and hope we can make it until the next paycheck. We just want to get the kids to school and fed and then to bed, with a little time left for TV."

And God is saying, "Come on! You can change your life! You can change your family! You can change your city! You can change your nation! You can change this world!"

But we offer excuses, "Lord, I can't even speak in a Bible study group. I can't even carry a tune. I can't even be disciplined enough to balance my checkbook. I can't even stop smoking." We think we are so limited, and it's all because of how we see ourselves.

The Weakest of the Weak

God said to Gideon, "You're going to save Israel."

Gideon said, "Oh no, not me. I can't because I'm from Manasseh."

Manasseh was the weakest tribe in Israel. You'd hear of the tribe of Judah and the Levites. But not Manasseh. They didn't even make it across Jordan. They stayed on the other side.

And furthermore, Gideon said, "I'm the least in my father's house." I'm the weakest of the weak.

But the angel said, "On the contrary, Gideon. You are a mighty man of valor."

The Weak Become Strong

Through a series of events, Gideon began to change his way of thinking. He rallied the troops of Israel and subdued the Midianites. The man who started out weak, poor, and scared rose to be one of the greatest judges and leaders in the history of Israel. He fulfilled his destiny. Where did it start? When an angel convinced him, "You're a mighty man of valor."

Change your self-image. Change how you see yourself. Listen to God's voice saying to you, "You are a mighty man or woman of valor. You are a person with a wonderful destiny."

"Well, I just can't seem to ever lose weight," you say. Well, wake up tomorrow morning and say, "I'm taking charge of this body. I'm going to be healthy and fit." You may say, "Well, I can't seem to get a better job." Tomorrow start saying, "I *can* have a better job." Believe that you can do what God says you can do. You are a mighty woman of valor. You are a mighty man of valor.

Same thing goes for bad habits. Do you bite your fingernails? Give that habit to God, draw on His strength, and see yourself conquering it. What about witnessing? You say you've never been good at evangelism? That's how you see yourself, not how God sees you. He says He will give us power and wisdom to testify for Him. Claim it. Then watch God bring in the spiritual harvest!

"Well, if all this is true," you ask, "then why do I have this sorry life I have now?" Because you're living with the results of what you have always believed about yourself. You're hiding in the wine press when God wants you charging the Midianites.

You're tending sheep on the back side of some mountain when God wants you in Pharaoh's face!

God said you are a mighty man of valor; you're a mighty woman of valor. When you believe you are what God says you are, you will be who God says you can be, you will have what God says you can have, and you will do what God says you can do. You will fulfill your destiny!

Steps to Your Destiny

1. What you think about yourself is one of the strongest controlling factors of your life. In what areas of your life do you still think negatively?

2. How you see yourself is how everyone else sees you. How do you see yourself?

3. Consider the trials and victories of Joseph, Moses, Gideon, and the children of Israel. How could you relate their experiences to your own life? Pick one obstacle in your life. With God's help, how can you begin to chip away at it? How can you beat it?

6

How to Renew Your Mind and Your Self-Image

There is no condemnation for those who are in Christ! When we come to Jesus, there is no more judgment, no more put downs, no more lowering of our self-image. There is no inferiority in Christ, and every thought that condemns us or makes us feel inferior is not of God.

> *There is therefore now no condemnation to those who are in Christ Jesus, who do not walk according to the flesh, but according to the Spirit. For the law of the Spirit of life in Christ Jesus has made me free from the law of sin and death. (Rom. 8:1-2)*

Steps to Renewing Your Self-Image

1. Capture and rid yourself of any thought that condemns you or makes you feel inferior.

Pull down those strongholds!

> *For the weapons of our warfare are not carnal but mighty in God for pulling down strongholds, casting down arguments and every high thing that exalts itself against the knowledge of God,*

> *bringing every thought into captivity to the obedience of Christ. (2 Cor. 10:4-5)*

Many of you still don't realize how powerful your thoughts are. Stop allowing your thoughts to condemn you. Stop allowing those negative thoughts to control you. Rid yourself of those thoughts! Conviction brings us to change, but condemnation paralyzes and binds us.

Begin to say, "I'm created in God's likeness and image. I'm a child of the King. I'm more than a conqueror. I'm an overcomer through Christ. This is the victory that overcomes the world, even my faith."

When the boss says, "We have a new opportunity. Would you like to step in?" and you think, "Oh, what if I fail? What if I'm not good enough? What if I can't do it?"—capture that thought and make it obey Christ!

Think instead, "I can do all things through Christ" (Phil. 4:13). Say, "Give me that new position. I can handle it. I'm able." Jesus will empower you. He will enable you. Capture and get rid of every thought that condemns, that makes you feel inferior.

DESTINY KEY

EVERY THOUGHT THAT CONDEMNS OR MAKES US FEEL INFERIOR IS NOT OF GOD.

Our country spends billions of dollars on weight-loss programs every year. It's because we feel inferior. The programs seldom work because change doesn't start in the body. It starts with our mind and our spirit. We must change our thoughts, then the weight will not be an issue. If we think there's no purpose or reason for our existence then we're going to feel inferior no matter how much we weigh; no matter how much hair we have; no matter how much money we have made; no matter what kind of job we have; no matter what kind of grades we make.

When you make your mind obedient to the Word of God, you will begin to think, "I am what God says I am. I can have what God says I can have. I can do what God says I can do."

2. Believe the love that God has for you.

> *And we have known and believed the love that God has for us. God is love, and he who abides in love abides in God, and God in him. (1 John 4:16)*

Can you believe the love God has for us? God loves us unconditionally with all that He is and all that He has. Do you believe that? People hear Scripture verses that say Jesus took our sickness and provided healing, that Jesus came to give abundant life. And the people respond to those verses by saying things like, "Well, that sounds too good to be true."

It's not too good to be true. It is true! Jesus isn't too good to be true. He *is* true! Salvation isn't too good to be true. It *is* true! Heaven isn't too good to be true. It *is* true!

I really believe that one day I will stand in the throne room of God and see His glory—seraphim, cherubim, Michael, Gabriel. I believe in the love that God has for me. I believe that God saw me before He created the world, before the foundations of the earth, and He chose me that I might be adopted as His son. I believe the love that God has for me.

Do I deserve it? Oh, no! Could I earn it? No way! Am I worthy of it? Never! But I believe the love God has for me. That's why He wants to prosper my life, bless my life, lift my life to the highest possible level—because He loves me. I don't deserve it. I can't earn it. I'm not worthy of it. He just loves me.

DESTINY KEY

GOD LOVES US UNCONDITIONALLY WITH ALL THAT HE IS AND ALL THAT HE HAS.

Now, you parents are the same way, aren't you? You have children, and, when they're little—two, three, and four years old—they stretch you all out of shape, exhaust you, and then want you to take care of them! They wake you up in the middle of the night and want you to feed them. And you do. They don't earn it. But you love them. And mothers, after these babies have stretched your stomach and spread your hips, you say, "Aren't you cute? I love you, you little

sweetie." And kids accept that love. They believe the love that parents have for them.

You'll never find your kid downstairs crying, "Oh, I'm just afraid that you're not going to let me eat today."

You would say to them, "What!?"

"I woke up afraid that you probably want me to suffer and that I couldn't have any Cheerios." They never think that way—at least mine don't. I find my little ones in the kitchen dragging the chair over to the cupboard.

I ask, "What are you doing?"

"I get the Cheerios."

They believe that it's all theirs. At age four my son, Micah, would climb up in my closet. I'd ask him what was he doing, and he would say, "Just looking."

I would say to him, "What are you looking for?"

"Whatever I want," he'd answer. He believed it was all his.

When a commercial for a toy comes on TV my kids call me, "Dad! Dad, quick, c'mere. Can I have that for Christmas?"

And I say, "Well . . . maybe . . . oh, sure." Inside I'm saying, "Man, I'd like to get that for them. I want them to have that." I love them, and they believe the love I have for them.

When we give a gift to our children, not once do they look at that present and say, "Oh, Dad, you shouldn't have gotten this for me. I can't believe it. Why did you do it? I'm not worthy of this. Dad, take it back. I'm sure it cost too much." I don't know about your kids, but I don't think that thought even crosses the minds of my children. They open those presents and say, "Thank you, Dad!"

Don't get me wrong. As a parent there are a lot of things I don't give to my children even though they ask. They can't have a snake just because they think it's pretty in the aquarium. They can't eat cookies all day long and no meat and fruits and vegetables. And they can't stay up late night after night, because little bodies need sleep. I know this better than they do. They may ask for these things, but they won't get them. I know better! A good father does not give his children harmful or hurtful things just because they ask for them. But he loves to give them good, positive, and productive things when they ask for them. And so does God!

When you read in the Bible that God wants to heal, just say, "That's the kind of God He is. I believe He can heal me!" And when the Bible says God wants to prosper us, instead of replying, "It's just too good to be true," say, "Yes! God can prosper my life." Let's believe the love that God has for us!

When something good happens, smile and say, "That's just like God. He loves me." Instead of, "Better watch out. When something good happens, something bad is right around the corner!" Let's get rid of that old, negative mentality. Believe the love that God has for you.

3. Believe that God has a destiny planned for your life.

As I said in Chapter 1, before the foundation of the world, I was on God's mind. Before I was in my mother's womb, I was on God's mind. You were on His mind too. He knew your name, your height, even your shoe size. He knew your wife or your husband. According to the good counsel of His will, He established a destiny plan for your life.

DESTINY KEY

ACCORDING TO THE GOOD COUNSEL OF HIS WILL, HE ESTABLISHED A DESTINY PLAN FOR YOUR LIFE.

I'm not deciding my destiny. I'm just doing the things God says to do, applying the principles the Bible says to apply, and discovering my destiny. I don't have to make it happen. I'm just taking paths that God selected and readied for me.

> *For we are His workmanship, created in Christ Jesus for good works, which God prepared beforehand that we should walk in them. (Eph. 2:10)*

God has a great plan for your future. Can you believe that? It's true! And it should make you want to get up and go. Remember Paul? They couldn't keep him down. After they beat and mocked him, he just kept getting up and heading after his destiny.

4. Remove the limitations from your mind.

In Psalm 78 we read that Israel had been miraculously brought out of Egypt. The Israelites came out with all the silver and gold and jewels of Egypt, all the wealth of the great nation that built the pyramids and the sphinx, the nation that had one of the most intricate languages and one of the greatest architecturally designed cities of the world. That great nation was totally ransacked and overtaken by a group of slaves—the nation of Israel.

> ***DESTINY KEY***
>
> THERE IS CONFIDENCE, THERE IS BOLDNESS, THERE IS JOY IN KNOWING GOD PLANNED YOUR LIFE.

When the Israelites went through the Red Sea, the whole army of Egypt drowned trying to retrieve its gold and silver. But what happened when Israel got out in the wilderness? They forgot about God's power. All the limitations and fears and worries that controlled their minds all those years as slaves began to control them again. Here they had guidance from a pillar of cloud by day and a pillar of fire by night, nourishing manna brought in *via airmail* every morning, and water flowing out of a rock, and yet they still wondered what would become of them.

> *How often they provoked Him in the wilderness,*
> *And grieved Him in the desert!*
> *Yes, again and again they tempted God,*
> *And limited the Holy One of Israel.*
> *They did not remember His power:*
> *The day when He redeemed them from the enemy. (Ps. 78:40-42)*

They didn't remember that God was with them to help them. So they died in the wilderness, and God was grieved. God isn't happy when we are defeated. God is grieved when we don't access His power in our life. So many of us accept jobs we don't like with incomes we don't like. We're not happy, but because of our feelings of inferiority and our limited mind-set, we say, "Oh

well, I'd better settle for what I have. There are a lot of folks who have less. So I'll just praise the Lord."

"Do you like your job?"

"No."

"Well, why don't you do something about it?"

"Because, we're supposed to just be content with what we have."

"But you're not content."

"I just thank God for what I have."

Now, it could be that God is teaching you to be content in all things, just as Paul learned to be. But it's more likely that you're in bondage because of the limitations in your own mind, rather than doing what you feel God put in your heart to do. You aren't believing in God's power. Let's remove all the limitations from our lives.

Being content in all situations is one thing. But if you're just existing, clinging to what's safe and familiar, that's another. Why spend your life trying to figure out what you *can't* do? Take a chance! Get out of the boat, man! Get out there with Jesus, woman! Sure, when you step out on the water you're going to sink once in a while or get the bottom of your robe wet, but at least you're out there. You'll be closer to Jesus than those back in the boat.

DESTINY KEY

AS LONG AS YOU SIT BACK, NOT BELIEVING GOD'S POWER IN YOUR LIFE, YOU'LL NEVER KNOW WHO YOU COULD REALLY BE OR WHAT YOU COULD DO.

Get out there and take some risks! Push your limits. The glorious thing is, when you do it and fulfill what God called you to do, you make that business work, or you make that family work, or you get that new position, or you start hearing God's voice during your quiet times, or you start loving that person you disliked. And you know what? In the process of doing these things, you'll likely wake up and find yourself right on course with your God-given destiny.

At that point, give all the glory to God for these things. He will be pleased and honored. The folks that always held you back and

told you to be careful and to slow down suddenly disappear. They'll be off trying to find someone else to discourage. But those who push back their limits honor and glorify God.

I refuse to settle for less than God's perfect will, His destiny path for me. I refuse to settle into some rut, some maintenance life—just to be another statistical norm or part of the average. We're human beings created in the likeness and image of God. We're given the power to have dominion. Take the limits off your mind. Go for it! As long as you sit back, not believing God's power in your life, you'll never know who you could really be or what you could do.

"But what if I fail?"

Oh, it's guaranteed you'll fail. At least a few times. It's just part of life. Failing is part of growing, but no failure is lasting unless when you fall down you stay down. Someone has aptly said, "We failed our way to victory." We try something that doesn't work, and we try again. Then we try another thing that doesn't work, and we try again. And we just keep trying until we find what works. So we shouldn't be afraid of failure. Destiny's path is crowded with failures on the way to victory.

The men who sold MS-DOS for a pittance thought they had a failure. The guy who bought it—Bill Gates—is still living on it and isn't doing too badly. There are many times that we fail our way to victory. But if our limits and boundaries are overly restrictive, if we keep a "be careful, watch out" attitude, we'll develop *hardening of the attitudes* until we die in mediocrity. Push back your limits!

The children of Israel limited God. Again and again they grieved God, the Holy One of Israel. And they died in the wilderness. Let's not repeat their mistake. Let's take the limits off!

5. Learn to like yourself no matter what state you're in.

This is easier said than done because we all tend to get down on ourselves. I want you to realize that you are not always going to do everything right, and you're not always going to have it all together. You already know that, but we try to deny it and we think, "If I could just get strong enough and good enough I'd

never have a bad day. I would just cruise through life, and everything would be great."

What I want to say to you is that you have to learn to like yourself even on the bad days. Even when your hair isn't right, you need to smile at the mirror. Put on a hat and go. Smile at yourself, feel good about yourself, and get on with it. Learn to like yourself no matter what state you're in.

> *Not that I speak in regard to need, for I have learned in whatever state I am, to be content. (Phil. 4:11)*

You have to *learn* this; it doesn't just come to you. And "contented" doesn't mean "satisfied." Paul was never satisfied. He was always pressing on, going for the prize, moving and growing in God. But he was content in whatever state he found himself—sitting in jail or sitting in the Temple; hanging on to a board, floating to shore after a shipwreck; if he had little, or if he had much. Whether he was controlled by the Roman government or chased by the Jews, he said, "I have learned to be content."

> *I know how to be abased, and I know how to abound. Everywhere and in all things I have learned both to be full and to be hungry, both to abound and to suffer need. I can do all things through Christ who strengthens me. (Phil. 4:12-13)*

So you made a mistake. Boy, you really messed up! You blew a deal and lost the commission and it's gone, history; it's over, and it's all your fault. Just grin and say, "That sure was stupid." Get out tomorrow and get a better deal, a bigger deal—and grow.

You hurt a friend's feelings? You said something really dumb? Confess it to God, apologize to your friend, and then go on. But don't sit around hating yourself.

You got a raise, and you're on the way home and so excited. Your car stereo is cranked up. Then you rear-end somebody. And you hate yourself. You call yourself an idiot. But you're the same person after the fender-bender as you were before.

When they gave you a pink slip and said you had been let go, for whatever reason, it didn't change who you are or the fact that God has a wonderful destiny arranged for you. So

don't let it change how you feel about yourself. You're the same person looking for a job as you were when the first company hired you and said you were the "greatest thing since apple pie." Yet the tendency is to say, "I'm so miserable. I don't have a job." Who wants to hire someone with an attitude like that? Believe in yourself. Feel good about yourself no matter what state you're in. Get out there and tell everybody how great you are, and that if they don't hire you they're going to miss a tremendous opportunity to prosper.

When they ask, "Well, who do you think you are?" say, "I think I'm one of the best things that's ever stepped into this office. Hire me, and I'll prove it." But if you go in and say, "Well, I lost my old job. You wouldn't want to hire me, would you?" you're displaying feelings of inferiority. Often, circumstances bring out these feelings of inferiority.

When you blame others for your circumstances—that boss who fired you, or the person who caused the automobile accident, or the economy for your lack of financial success, or the government for your tax problem—what's happening is that the circumstances are bringing out the poor self-image that's been there all the time. A poor self-image is like a tea bag, and the circumstances of life are just the hot water being poured over you. Out seeps that poor self-image.

But when you feel good about yourself, it doesn't matter whether you have a fender-bender or lose a job, or whether the economy goes down and taxes go up. None of those things change who you are. When you believe in yourself, no matter what the circumstances, you will get up every morning and say, "I am a blessing going somewhere to happen." You forget about anybody that you could blame or point your finger at because you don't have time to think about those folks. You're out there doing what God called you to do.

Don't think that walking with God means every day is going to be glorious. Some days He will send you through the "valley of the shadow of death," and you're going to look into that valley and say, "God, are You sure that is the way? I don't feel too good about myself in there." And God will say, "I don't want you to camp there. I just want you to walk through it." Feel good about

yourself whether you're lying beside still waters, frolicking in green grass, or walking through the valley.

Do you know that it's "in the presence of your enemies" that God prepares a great table for you? Those are some of the best times. When it seems everything is against you, when you have enemies and problems and darkness all around you; when you've fought some tremendous battles and experienced some defeats and some challenges—that's when He prepares that glorious banquet.

6. Rejoice and be thankful for who God has made you to be.

> *But let each one examine his own work, and then he will have rejoicing in himself alone, and not in another. For each one shall bear his own load. (Gal. 6:4-5)*

Wendy taught me this verse, and she preaches it to me quite regularly. Examine your own work and have rejoicing in yourself alone. Be thankful for who you are, and don't worry about anyone else. If you're always wishing you could be someone else, you will never fulfill your destiny. And even if you could be somebody else, you wouldn't be happy.

How many times has the story been told about the pauper who wished he could become royalty and the prince who wished he could be a commoner? You cannot be happy wishing you were someone else. Rejoice and be thankful for who God has made you to be.

Someone once said to me, "Pastor, I wish I could preach like you. I wish I could do what you do." I looked at him and said, "No, you don't. First of all, you don't know what I do. You only see me one out of 168 hours a week. You might not like the other 167 hours. You don't want to be me. Be yourself and rejoice. Be thankful for who God has made you to be."

Don't look at the singer or the instrumentalist and say, "Oh, I wish I could do what they do." Even if you could do what they do, you might not like it. You do what God has called you to do. If you are thankful for what God has put in your life, you will rejoice in yourself and find fulfillment. Sometimes you have to

do it by faith. Sometimes you just have to do it because you know it's right. But after you do it, you begin to feel it.

Do you know how much power is released in your life through gratitude? Go through the Bible sometime and look at all the Scriptures that have to do with being thankful. In Philippians 4:6-7, Paul said:

> *In everything by prayer and supplication, with thanksgiving, let your requests be made known to God; and the peace of God . . . will guard your hearts and minds through Christ Jesus.*

Paul said in 1 Thessalonians 5:18, "In everything give thanks; for this is the will of God in Christ Jesus for you."

Thank God that you can be a salesperson, a businessperson, a homemaker, a manager, a teacher, or a peewee league coach. Thank Him for gifting your hands to build or to repair or to paint. Thank Him for what He has made you and gifted you to be.

DESTINY KEY

BE YOURSELF AND REJOICE. BE THANKFUL FOR WHO GOD HAS MADE YOU TO BE.

When you're thankful—"Thank You, Lord, for my family and my children. Thank You that I can be a godly parent"—God says, "I will bless you. I will prosper you. I will increase you." Gratitude releases greater power and greater blessing in your life. Rejoice in yourself.

Your mind takes you in whatever direction in which you have focused your thoughts. Those who have experience with airplanes will know that there are devices called transponders at various locations all over the United States and the world. An airplane is designed with a computer and a specific radar and radio system that locks into these transponders.

If I'm heading for Los Angeles, as soon as I get in the air, I lock in my course based on the signal that I'm getting from transponders in Portland, Eugene, Redding, San Francisco, and then finally in Los Angeles. So the plane's automatic pilot keeps me on course based on where the next signal is coming from.

The transponder for Seattle is southeast of the city outside a small town called Enumclaw. When you're coming into Seattle you have to click off the automatic pilot several miles away, because the airport isn't in Enumclaw. Wherever that transponder is, that's where the airplane heads as long as it's on automatic pilot.

Similarly, your mind is focused on something. It may be focused on getting by or just hanging in there and getting the bills paid. That may be all you can see for your future. You may have gotten married with the thought in the back of your mind, "This probably won't last, and I can always get a divorce and find somebody else." These beliefs are your mind's transponders, and your life will head in the direction of those beliefs.

Your thoughts may not even be conscious thoughts. But in the dark recesses of your mind, you believe a certain way, you think certain thoughts, and these thoughts are your mind's homing device. Whatever you have focused your thoughts on is what you're moving toward. The problem is, you may not like it when you get there.

One of the greatest things about being a child of God is that after salvation, we can renew our minds. We can place our thoughts where we want them to be, focus our thoughts on higher and better things, and move in that direction—toward our destiny.

What will you be like when you're sixty? Do you have a picture of yourself, your home, your life, your bank account? Where do you want to be when you're seventy? Do you have a picture of it yet? How will you look? How will you stand? How will you walk? What will you do? What kind of house will you have? What kind of life will you live? When Billy Graham was seventy-four, *Time* magazine asked him about his retirement. His reply? "I can't find 'retirement' in the Bible. I have no plans to retire."

Few people have a plan for greater things in their last days. They spend their whole life learning and growing and gaining wisdom so they can drive a motor home to Phoenix. Focus on where you're going and what you're going to do in the years ahead. The future is yours. Make it. Shape it. Mold it. Live it. Don't just hang in there. Don't just go through it. Make it what you want it to be.

Steps to Your Destiny

What are your thoughts concerning renewing your self-image?

1. Capture and rid yourself of any thought that condemns you or makes you feel inferior.

2. Believe in the love God has for you.

3. Believe that God has a destiny planned for your life.

4. Remove the limitations from your mind.

5. Learn to like yourself no matter what state you're in.

6. Rejoice and be thankful for who God has made you to be.

7

Seven Powerful Forces That Flow from Following Destiny

We've seen that without a sense of destiny, life is empty. Now let's look at what happens in life when you *know* that you have a purpose and a destiny. How will this knowledge affect you? What will it produce in you? When a person has a sense of destiny, powerful forces are released in his or her life. In this chapter, we'll look at seven forces that flow from a sense of destiny.

People with a Sense of Destiny Have Vision

Proverbs 29:18 says, "Where there is no vision, the people perish" (KJV). When a person lacks vision, it likely means that he lacks a sense of destiny. To draw on our football analogy from Chapter 1, he lacks a sense of direction to the goal line, so he has no vision of where to run and where not to run to score. He ends up losing.

Without a vision, which comes from a sense of destiny, people "perish." But when they know there is a purpose for their lives, they will begin to *see* portions of their future. They get a vision for their lives. I don't mean in some weird, mystical way, as a New Age guru might suggest, but they will have a sense of direction and focus that allows them to see where they are going

in life. Remember, *vision is an ability to generally anticipate, imagine, or foresee experiences and developments you want to participate in or avoid as you move on destiny's course.*

At nineteen years of age, I began to sense that my destiny was to help people, to minister to their needs, and to teach them the Bible. At age twenty-two I began to see how I would do that, at least in part. I had a vision of pastoring a church, teaching in the media, and building ministries within the church that would serve people in practical ways. My wife, Wendy, shared this vision, and at age twenty-four, Wendy and I started Christian Faith Center. Our vision became a reality. It continues to unfold and grow as we move forward together in our destinies.

DESTINY KEY

WHERE THERE IS NO VISION, PEOPLE PERISH.

Once we begin to think positively about our life and future, we begin to see positive things and have a vision for the blessings of God. If we have no sense of destiny, it is nearly impossible to think positively and have a vision for anything good. We begin to think we are just accidents going somewhere to happen.

Most high-school graduates (and in many cases, college graduates) come out of school with no vision. They have knowledge; they have information. But most of them were not taught the principles of destiny, so they have no sense of purpose or vision. "Where there is no vision, the people perish."

I meet with the junior-high and high-school kids at Christian Faith School about once a month. My purpose is to inspire them to discover their destiny in God. They are learning why they were born and what God has planned for their lives. They know they are not an accident of evolution or just the fateful result of a sexual union. They are part of God's family, and they have a divine destiny. If they make good, God-led choices, they will fulfill and enjoy that destiny. If they choose to do their own thing, they may miss the greatest life possible.

Vision is like a snapshot of your future and your destiny. It enables you to see where you are going and what you will be doing. If the camera is out of focus, the image may be blurry and the subject indistinguishable. Many people have a blurry focus on their future. They are just wandering aimlessly through life, hoping that something good will happen but expecting that it won't.

As you seek the Lord and begin to learn about yourself, two simultaneous events happen. You are discovering your destiny. And as God leads you, you are choosing a path—a vision is becoming clear. Vision encompasses both God's plan and your decisions. "For we are God's fellow workers" (1 Cor. 3:9).

> *Then the* LORD *answered me and said:*
> *"Write the vision*
> *And make it plain on tablets,*
> *That he may run who reads it.*
> *For the vision is yet for an appointed time;*
> *But at the end it will speak, and it will not lie.*
> *Though it tarries, wait for it;*
> *Because it will surely come,*
> *It will not tarry." (Hab. 2:2-3)*

You need to write down what you are focusing on as a vision for your life. Don't fear that it might change—it probably will. And don't get long and flowery. Make it plain and simple so that you are forced to be real. Many times we make our vision so romantic that it can never come to pass, and we disappoint ourselves. We're not talking about creating fantasies here. We're discussing a vision for your life. Get down to the nitty-gritty of what you feel God is saying to you and what you want for your future. Together, you and the Lord will develop a picture that will be sharply focused and will put you—and keep you—on the path of your destiny.

DESTINY KEY

DISCIPLINE IS A PRODUCT OF PURPOSE AND GOALS AND DESTINY.

People with a Sense of Destiny Have Discipline

My main source of exercise and refreshment is bicycling. Wendy and I have ridden thousands of miles across our state and the Northwest. I love tinkering with bikes and their components. I've built my bikes from piles of parts, and I enjoy keeping them in perfect condition. Over the years, I've noticed one thing to be consistently true. When I have a specific goal, such as a 150-mile ride over two mountains, I am more disciplined in my riding.

Goals are: *specific accomplishments, skills, and events (mileposts on destiny's course) that you desire to achieve.*

Discipline is a product of *purpose* and goals and destiny. Purpose, as used in this book, is: *the reason you do what you do.*

When I have no purpose—no specific reason for riding my bike—I ride around casually and don't push it. But when I have a purpose in my riding—to get stronger and faster and thus achieve personal satisfaction—I get motivated to work hard, ride long distances, and push myself to the limit so I'll be ready to conquer more mountains.

Most people lack discipline in their lives because they have no goals, no sense of destiny. They struggle with their weight, for example. Yet when they try to *do* something about it, their motivation lasts about two weeks—after which there is another piece of exercise equipment piled up in the spare room and another stack of bills for diet programs that didn't work. The problem isn't the equipment or the program. *The problem is lack of discipline that comes from no sense of destiny.*

If you know your destiny was established by God before the foundation of the world, you have a reason to live life to the fullest and make the most of every moment. When you have a goal, you have the motivation. The young man who doesn't want to comb his hair or brush his teeth becomes the neatest dude in town when he wants to get close to a particular young woman. Suddenly, he has the discipline that Mom could never get him to have, because now he has a sense of purpose. His purpose is immediate: to get that girl's attention. His goal: a date. And the destiny he longs for is more long term: to marry and live happily ever after.

It's hard to get through classes, homework, and studies unless you have a purpose and a long-term sense of destiny. As a high-school student, I barely did enough to get by, because I considered most of what we did irrelevant and I had no purpose. But as a college student, I had discovered my destiny: to be a minister. My purpose soon followed: make good grades and learn as much as I could to help me in my long-term destiny. The result? I became much more disciplined in my studies. I ended up with a 3.97 grade-point average and became valedictorian of my class. For me, an immediate purpose and a long-term destiny made me disciplined. It will you too.

It's all a question of "why." If I have a destiny and a purpose, I have *reasons* to live right, to stay holy and clean, to pray and study the Word. I have a reason to discipline myself.

Young people have no motivation to keep their bodies pure and to avoid sexual immorality if they think they are just products of evolution. With that kind of thinking, why shouldn't they have sex? Especially if it brings short-term closeness and feelings of love. It's only when they know that they are God's children and that sex is a part of the blood covenant they will have with their spouse that they realize that sexual purity has a purpose. Knowing that, they will have the discipline to refrain from premarital sex.

DESTINY KEY

DISCIPLINE THAT FLOWS OUT OF A SENSE OF DESTINY IS REWARDING.

Christians who have no sense of destiny try to live right for legalistic and religious reasons. They try to have discipline without understanding their destiny. They don't enjoy life because they don't have a purpose for what they are doing. Their children usually rebel against their religious upbringing because there is no fulfillment in it.

But discipline that flows out of a sense of destiny is rewarding. There is a sense of satisfaction, because I am reaching for my destiny and pleasing the Lord.

Let's see if I can tie together some things we've just covered. You recall my love of biking? Well, I can endure the muscle pain (the discipline) of riding my bike to the peak of the mountain (my

goal), because I know it will make me a better cyclist, bring health and self-satisfaction (my purpose), and prepare me for even more challenging rides on wonderful, unexplored mountain roads (my destiny). Along the way, I imagine the view from the peak. I think about how great it will feel to catch my breath, relax, gulp from my water bottle, and chat with my wife (this is my vision, which helps get me to the top).

Paul liked athletic metaphors too:

> *Do you not know that those who run in a race all run, but one receives the prize? Run in such a way that you may obtain it. And everyone who competes for the prize is temperate in all things. Now they do it to obtain a perishable crown, but we for an imperishable crown. Therefore I run thus: not with uncertainty. Thus I fight: not as one who beats the air. But I discipline my body and bring it into subjection, lest, when I have preached to others, I myself should become disqualified.* (1 Cor. 9:24-27)

Discipline is a powerful force for good in our lives. It doesn't always come easily, and it almost never comes without a sense of purpose and destiny. But Paul and you and I—we all have God-given destinies. We are chasing the crowns of glory God has for us. If that's not worth bringing our bad habits and slothful minds and out-of-shape bodies "into subjection" for, if that's not worth becoming more disciplined for, then tell me—what is?

People with a Sense of Destiny Have Self-Esteem

When we don't believe in ourselves, we don't function at our highest level. The lack of self-esteem in our world is manifested in the enormous number of people on welfare. Immorality and marital failures are also evidences of this problem. Feeling insecure or inferior makes me defensive, angry, selfish and jealous of others. All these characteristics are prevalent in our society. But when I know who I am, when I know I have a destiny from the Lord, my self-esteem rises, and my lifestyle reflects it.

Many of our societal problems are due to the breakdown of our value systems and the erosion of our self-esteem. When we have sex outside of marriage or we divorce our spouse because

the marriage vows are too tough, we lose our sense of dignity, pride, and self-worth. When we drink or use drugs because it is "socially acceptable," or when we believe ourselves to be accidents of evolution, we have little self-esteem. If our desire is for a socialist government to take care of all our needs, we lose our sense of dignity and pride. Satan has promoted these philosophies in our society today, and the results are apparent. Crime, unwanted pregnancies, abortion, divorce, sickness, depression—all these are manifestations of the low self-esteem of individuals in our society.

> ***DESTINY KEY***
>
> WHEN I HAVE A SENSE OF DESTINY FROM THE LORD, MY SELF-ESTEEM RISES, AND MY LIFESTYLE REFLECTS IT.

Religion has been one source of the problem in the past years. Angry preachers and misguided churches have contributed to a negative self-image and anxiety in many Christians. Christians are not often known for their confidence, openness, leadership, or positive outlook. Although there are many exceptions to this rule, in general, the world views the church as negative, fearful, condemning, and controlling.

But when we go to the Word of God, we see mankind as highly regarded. God created us, of all creatures, to be the most similar to Himself. In Psalm 8:3-6, we read:

When I consider Your heavens, the work of Your fingers,
The moon and the stars, which You have ordained,
What is man that You are mindful of him,
And the son of man that You visit him?
For You have made him a little lower than the angels,
And You have crowned him with glory and honor.
You made him to have dominion over the works of Your hands;
You have put all things under his feet.

The prophet Jeremiah wrote that God has good thoughts toward us—thoughts of peace—and He has given us a future (Jer. 29:11). When we turn our thoughts to what God says about

us, we begin to feel good. We have the confidence to do what He created us to do.

A child who is ridiculed, condemned, or told he is no good and will never amount to anything will probably believe his critics and fulfill that portrayal. The words of friends, parents, teachers, preachers, and others become *software data* in the *computer* of a child's mind. If she doesn't know what God says about her, she believes what everyone else says. That child will be bound by that self-image until someone helps her renew her mind with God's Word.

Maybe you were abused and wrongly taught about your own personhood. Right now, truth from the Bible can set you free from the limiting, controlling negatives in your mind (John 8:31-32). If you will accept what God says and believe you are who He says you are, then you can be on your way to a new life and a fulfilling destiny.

Look what else God thinks and says about you:

> *God stands in the congregation of the mighty;*
> *He judges among the gods. . . .*
> *I said, "You are gods,*
> *And all of you are children of the Most High." (Ps. 82:1, 6)*

> *For God so loved the world that He gave His only begotten Son, that whoever believes in Him should not perish but have everlasting life. (John 3:16)*

> *No longer do I call you servants, for a servant does not know what his master is doing; but I have called you friends, for all things that I heard from My Father I have made known to you. You did not choose Me, but I chose you and appointed you that you should go and bear fruit, and that your fruit should remain, that whatever you ask the Father in My name He may give you. (John 15:15-16)*

> *What then shall we say to these things? If God is for us, who can be against us? He who did not spare His own Son, but delivered Him up for us all, how shall He not with Him also freely give us all things? (Rom. 8:31-32)*

> *Who shall separate us from the love of Christ? Shall tribulation, or distress, or persecution, or famine, or nakedness, or peril, or sword? As it is written: "For Your sake we are killed all day long; we are accounted as sheep for the slaughter." Yet in all these things we are more than conquerors through Him who loved us. (Rom. 8:35-37)*

> *For we are His workmanship, created in Christ Jesus for good works, which God prepared beforehand that we should walk in them. (Eph. 2:10)*

> *For it is God who works in you both to will and to do for His good pleasure. (Phil. 2:13)*

> *And my God shall supply all your need according to His riches in glory by Christ Jesus. (Phil. 4:19)*

> *We love Him because He first loved us. (1 John 4:19)*

As we renew our minds to these truths, we replace thoughts of inferiority, insecurity, and shame with thoughts of competence, assurance, and self-worth. In Romans 12:2, Paul says:

> *And do not be conformed to this world, but be transformed by the renewing of your mind, that you may prove what is that good and acceptable and perfect will of God.*

We will live the will of God when our mind accepts what He thinks about us and not what we may have been taught by others or concluded on our own.

As you get a sense of destiny, you will begin to feel valued; you will have a sense of self-worth, self-esteem, and confidence. You were created for a purpose. God established a great destiny for you, and you have what it takes to fulfill that destiny. Don't let your past, your failures, or your pain bring you to a place of discouragement. Believe in yourself—you are who God says you are.

People with a Sense of Destiny Have Faith and Courage

God created you. God has established a future for you. God has gifted you to fulfill your destiny. Your situation is like that of the apostle Paul. Paul knew that God had destined him to preach the gospel to the Gentiles and to be a witness of Jesus before kings. Through every trial and challenge, that sense of destiny motivated, encouraged, and kept him going. His was not an easy road. God had shown him the things he must suffer to fulfill his destiny (Acts 9:15-16).

But faith and courage rise up in the hearts of people of destiny. You may be excited about what God has for you, but don't think your destiny course will be a "happy trail." The Christian life is the greatest life we can experience, but it is not necessarily the easiest. The point is that like Paul you'll have the faith and courage to endure tribulation if you realize that you're on course with your destiny. The runner can go through the pain and the hardships of training if he focuses on the prize of winning the race.

In 2 Corinthians 4, Paul writes of the difficulties of living out his destiny and the spirit of faith that took him through.

> *We are hard pressed on every side, yet not crushed; we are perplexed, but not in despair; persecuted, but not forsaken; struck down, but not destroyed. (2 Cor. 4:8-9)*

> *And since we have the same spirit of faith, according to what is written, "I believed and therefore I spoke," we also believe and therefore speak. (2 Cor. 4:13)*

> *Therefore we do not lose heart. Even though our outward man is perishing, yet the inward man is being renewed day by day. For our light affliction, which is but for a moment, is working for us a far more exceeding and eternal weight of glory, while we do not look at the things which are seen, but at the things which are not seen. For the things which are seen are temporary, but the things which are not seen are eternal. (2 Cor. 4:16-18)*

We must have a spirit of faith if we are to make it to the end of our course. Paul said, "I have fought the good fight, I have finished the race, I have kept the faith" (2 Tim. 4:7). We cannot finish what God has set before us with a negative, pessimistic, or fearful attitude. We must obey the command of Jesus to "have faith in God" (Mark 11:22) and believe His word in every situation. When the storms come, when the enemy arises, when friends desert us, when sickness comes, when finances are short—have faith in God.

> ***DESTINY KEY***
>
> FAITH AND COURAGE RISE IN THE HEARTS OF PEOPLE OF DESTINY.

Many people have no reason to develop their faith. They live mundane lives and are not planning to do anything but get by—spiritually, physically, emotionally, and financially. But when you have a sense of destiny for yourself, your family, your business, or your ministry, you begin to have a desire and a drive to develop your faith.

Seoul, Korea's David (Paul) Yonggi Cho, pastor of the largest church in the world, said to me, "When you have vision, faith will rise almost automatically." It is virtually a simultaneous process. As your sense of destiny grows, as your vision grows, as your purpose grows, as your discipline grows, so also will your faith in God grow.

There are four things you can do to help your faith grow:

1. Read and study the Word.

So then faith comes by hearing, and hearing by the word of God. (Rom. 10:17)

Be diligent to present yourself approved to God, a worker who does not need to be ashamed, rightly dividing the word of truth. (2 Tim. 2:15)

2. Meditate on the Word and on God's destiny for your life.

This Book of the Law shall not depart from your mouth, but you shall meditate in it day and night, that you may observe to do

according to all that is written in it. For then you will make your way prosperous, and then you will have good success. (Josh. 1:8)

3. Confess God's Word daily.

So Jesus answered and said to them, "Have faith in God. For assuredly, I say to you, whoever says to this mountain, 'Be removed and be cast into the sea,' and does not doubt in his heart, but believes that those things he says will be done, he will have whatever he says." (Mark 11:22-23).

And since we have the same spirit of faith, according to what is written, "I believed and therefore I spoke," we also believe and therefore speak. (2 Cor. 4:13)

4. Spend time with people of faith who are seeking their destinies.

He who walks with wise men will be wise,
But the companion of fools will be destroyed. (Prov. 13:20)

Where there is no counsel, the people fall;
But in the multitude of counselors there is safety.
(Prov. 11:14)

God would not call you to do something—He would not set before you a destiny—and then not give you the support you need to accomplish it. But God will not do it for you. You must go for it in faith. God says that:

- "Faith is the substance of things hoped for." (Heb. 11:1)
- "Without faith it is impossible to please Him." (Heb. 11:6)
- "The victory that has overcome the world [is] our faith." (1 John 5:4)

The Scriptures above indicate that we have a responsibility to walk in faith. God goes further to say that people of destiny must:

- "Take it [the kingdom of God] by force." (Matt. 11:12)
- "Live by faith." (Rom. 1:17)

- "Walk by faith." (2 Cor. 5:7)
- "Fight the good fight of faith." (1 Tim. 6:12)

None of that sounds passive to me. Does it to you? No one achieves his or her destiny just sitting on the bench waiting for God to hit a home run. Instead, God gives us the bat and says, "Now get up to the plate; if you'll just swing, that ball will fly!" Faith is getting off the bench and stepping up to the plate. Many Christians have fallen short of their life's destiny because they worry what will happen if they step up to the plate. They hold back, doubt the Word, and tighten up on the inside.

Throughout Jesus' ministry on earth He told people it was their faith that made them whole, opened their eyes, and changed their lives. He was always pointing to the faith of people like Bartimaeus, the woman with an issue of blood, and the four who brought their friend to Jesus on a stretcher. It was obviously God's will that these people should be healed, but if it hadn't been for the faith of the people, nothing would have happened.

As you sense your destiny and the plan of God for your life, you will grow in faith and courage. Others may not understand how you can believe what you believe or do what you do, but remember—it comes from a sense of destiny. You know that God has already promised you that if you step to the plate, the ball will fly off that bat and over the fence.

Through the years of ministry at Christian Faith Center, I've stepped out in faith several times. We started construction on a 2,500-seat sanctuary with no money; we went on television when we hadn't finished the sanctuary; we started a liberal arts college from nothing; we started building a 60,000-square-foot ministry center with no money. Some people thought I had gone off the deep end, but in each case I knew I was moving toward our church's destiny. It wasn't my thing—it was God's thing, so faith was not a problem. I've launched a few projects that were not of God, and believing in them became a struggle. Eventually I abandoned them. But when you know you're in the will of God, faith rises.

People with a Sense of Destiny Have Resources

God's will is God's bill. God does not have a resource problem, and if we walk with Him in our destiny, we won't have a resource problem either. If we need more patience to complete a task, God's storehouse will open and He'll serve it up. If what we need to complete our destiny is more rest, God will see that it is provided. If what we need to complete our task is dedicated employees or personnel, we can expect them to come. And if what we need to start a new business or to home-school our children or to go on a mission trip or to start a new ministry or church—if what we need is money—*God's will is God's bill.* He can more than adequately meet any money needs.

Dr. Ed Cole, founder and president of the Christian Men's Network, says, "Money always follows ministry." When in the business or ministry to which God has called me, I'll have the resources I need. When I'm doing my own thing, I may go broke. I may have no rest; I may have no people; I may have no patience! You see, my will is my bill, but God's will is God's bill.

The Bible is full of God's promises to meet our needs and to provide abundantly for us.

> *And my God shall supply all your need according to His riches in glory by Christ Jesus. (Phil. 4:19)*

> *I have come that they may have life, and that they may have it more abundantly. (John 10:10)*

> *And you shall remember the* LORD *your God, for it is He who gives you power to get wealth, that He may establish His covenant which He swore to your fathers, as it is this day. (Deut. 8:18)*

> *And God is able to make all grace abound toward you, that you, always having all sufficiency in all things, may have an abundance for every good work. (2 Cor. 9:8)*

God gives us the power to get resources—spiritual, emotional and physical—so we can fulfill the destiny that He has for our lives. If we trust Him and walk with Him, there will be no lack

or shortage in our lives. I'm not saying that everything will be easy, but we should not always be struggling as we move forward in our life's calling.

Because most Christians are trying to "make a living" instead of living out their destiny, they never tap into the resources of heaven. God said He would meet our need according to "His riches in glory," not according to our lack on earth. As ambassadors of Christ (2 Cor. 5:20), we're funded by the abundance of heaven rather than the economy of earth.

DESTINY KEY

GOD GIVES US THE POWER TO GET RESOURCES SO WE CAN FULFILL THE DESTINY THAT HE HAS FOR OUR LIVES.

When Americans are sent to a foreign nation to serve as ambassadors, they do not live under the control or the economy of the nation in which they live. As ambassadors of the United States, they have the prosperity of our country behind them and they live in our economy. As Christians we can live from God's abundant supply as we serve Him and fulfill His plan for our lives. He can and will send the resources we need. It's up to God to fulfill His promises. It's up to us to trust Him!

Some Christians have been taught that prosperity is evil. I don't believe that. That kind of teaching has kept portions of the church poor, stagnant, and negative. While some Christians do nothing because they want to be piously poor, much of the world prospers and uses resources for selfish reasons. With more money we could build more churches, send more missionaries, establish more Christian colleges, and change the world.

Paul said, "The *love* of money is a root of all kinds of evil" (1 Tim. 6:10), but those who are rich should trust God and use their money for godly things. He never said poverty was a universal requisite for believers. He recognized that resources are needed to do what the Lord has destined us to do. Because of our poverty mentality, some of us have avoided our responsibility. For some, living in poverty is a great excuse for doing nothing. We don't send our kids to Christian schools, we don't help build our sanctuaries, we don't erect great colleges, and we don't affect

other nations because "we can't afford it." We have a built-in excuse for doing nothing to fulfill the Great Commission.

It goes without saying that we need more than just money to do God's will and fulfill His Great Commission. We need God's spiritual fruit in our life; we need the power of His Spirit moving in us; and we need each other. Money, however, is also usually needed. Let me share with you some principles that will help you as you seek to prosper financially for the glory of Christ's kingdom.

The Six Steps of God's Financial Program

1. Believe that God can bring prosperity to your life if you walk with Him.

If you are willing and obedient, you shall eat the good of the land. (Isa.1:19)

2. Give 10 percent of your income to your local church.

"Will a man rob God? Yet you have robbed Me! But you say, 'In what way have we robbed You?' In tithes and offerings. You are cursed with a curse, for you have robbed Me, even this whole nation. Bring all the tithes into the storehouse, that there may be food in My house, and try Me now in this," says the LORD of hosts, "If I will not open for you the windows of heaven and pour out for you such blessing that there will not be room enough to receive it." (Mal. 3:8-10)

3. Surpass your tithe with offerings as you are led by the Spirit.

He who sows sparingly will also reap sparingly, and he who sows bountifully will also reap bountifully. So let each one give as he purposes in his heart, not grudgingly or of necessity; for God loves a cheerful giver. (2 Cor. 9:6-7)

4. Know how your resources will advance your destiny.

For we are His workmanship, created in Christ Jesus for good works, which God prepared beforehand that we should walk in them. (Eph. 2:10)

5. Work hard and wise, knowing God will bless those things to which you set your hands.

If anyone will not work, neither shall he eat. (2 Thess. 3:10)

Blessed is the man
Who walks not in the counsel of the ungodly,
Nor stands in the path of sinners,
Nor sits in the seat of the scornful;
But his delight is in the law of the LORD,
And in His law he meditates day and night.
He shall be like a tree
Planted by the rivers of water,
That brings forth its fruit in its season,
Whose leaf also shall not wither;
And whatever he does shall prosper. (Ps. 1:1-3)

6. Be a wise steward of what you have now.

He who is faithful in what is least is faithful also in much; and he who is unjust in what is least is unjust also in much. (Luke 16:10)

When you are convinced of God's destiny for your life, you will have no trouble believing that God will provide the finances to get you there. If all you want to do is make a living, then do what most people in America do: get a job (or sign up for welfare). Get all you can, hang on to all you can, and don't let anyone rip you off. You'll make it through life. But if you want to prosper and move toward fulfilling your destiny, follow these principles and realize that money is just one of many tools—along with character, people, ideas, and other important components—to aid you on your course of destiny.

In Matthew 12:35, Jesus said:

> *"A good man out of the good treasure of his heart brings forth good things, and an evil man out of the evil treasure brings forth evil things."*

The issue is not what is around you—it's what is in you. If you have the vision, discipline, self-worth, faith, and courage that flow from a sense of destiny, you will bring forth whatever resources—emotionally, spiritually or physically—that it takes to see your destiny accomplished.

In every realm of life, the "treasure" that is in me greatly influences what happens around me. I can't blame my circumstances on the government, the economy, the environment, or anything else. If I have a clear sense of destiny, it will come forth, and nothing can stop that. The money, the people, the love, the joy, the patience, the ideas, the understanding—they all will come.

People with a Sense of Destiny Have Drive and Motivation

For years I thought there was something wrong with me. People seemed to move slowly and get very little done. Conversely, most people around me were frustrated at the pace I set and felt that I didn't like or appreciate them. I constantly wondered why people lived the way they did and never "moved on" with God. It seemed to me that the world was mediocre and that most people didn't want to live any other way.

Then I realized: I'm not crazy. It's just that most people have no sense of destiny. They get up in the morning to make a living, not to fulfill a destiny. They have no purpose other than to pay the mortgage, buy a new TV, keep a job, and make it until next month. That's why they feel *blah* about life.

Studies say more than 75 percent of Americans dislike their jobs. More than 70 percent suffer from depression or some form of anxiety. Every day Americans take thousands of antidepressants and tranquilizers. Why?

With the knowledge, skills, and opportunities we have in our modern society, you'd think we'd be the most excited people in

the history of the world. But when you look at the faces on the freeway every morning or into the heart of the average person, you don't find excitement. You find depression, boredom, and frustration.

A lack of purpose is to blame and, on a larger scale, a lack of destiny. We don't have a deep motivating drive to do our jobs well or to grow. We work to get by, and getting by isn't very exciting or motivating. When we get a sense of a higher calling in life—a purpose established by God before the foundation of the world—a destiny that He has set for us—then we can get excited, enthused, and motivated *every morning.*

DESTINY KEY

MY DESTINY MUST BE TRANSLATED INTO GOALS THAT GIVE ME A REASON TO GET UP AND GO TO WORK EVERY DAY.

As a teenager I had no Christian training and no vision for my future. The most fearful day of my life was the day of my high-school graduation, because I had no idea where I was going or what I would do with my life. I felt lost and consequently unmotivated. I'd say to my mother, "There's nothing to do." When she would suggest various activities, from cleaning the barn to fixing the fence, I would groan and try to ignore her. Without vision, a person wanders aimlessly and without motivation.

Our cities are full of people with great potential who probably will never get out of their environment, because the young people there are not being taught they have a potential destiny in God. They hang out at the street corner, bored, because they feel useless and have no purpose. No amount of government subsidies, no welfare or educational program will motivate or change a person who has no vision, purpose, or destiny.

My destiny must be translated into goals that give me a reason to get up and go to work every day. The finish line is the *life goal* or *grand finale* that I am striving for, but every day I take small steps that keep me moving toward the finish line. If I do not have daily goals and steps that I can take on a regular basis, I have not yet clarified my destiny. It's still foggy, or I'm just on a fantasy

trip and have no intention of finishing my life's course. Make the vision clear and plain (Hab. 2:2-3). Write it down in simple steps that you can start on today. This will begin the motivation process that will build and intensify until it carries you all the way to the finish line.

The word *enthused* comes from two Greek words: *in* and *theos*. It means "to be in God." If you are in God, in God's will, in God's destiny plan for your life, you will be excited and motivated! There is no greater motivation than to realize that you are doing what God established for you to do before the foundation of the world. When you wake up every day, you know that God has great things for you to accomplish, and all you have to do is walk in paths that He prearranged and made ready for you (Eph. 2:10).

You will have no problem being motivated when you focus on the destiny God has established for you. No matter what area of work you feel the Lord has called you to, it will be exciting and motivating to you because you will be "in God," *in theos*, enthused with the power of traveling your destiny course.

I know computer analysts who are excited every day of their lives. I know homemakers, teachers, administrators, technicians, and builders who are motivated by a sense of destiny and purpose that keeps them going toward the finish line. You too can be energized, driven, and motivated by the power of traveling destiny's course.

> *[Not in your own strength] for it is God Who is all the while effectually at work in you [energizing and creating in you the power and desire], both to will and to work for His good pleasure and satisfaction and delight. (Phil. 2:13, Amplified)*

God wants to energize you with a sense of destiny and purpose. Like a runner who only sees the finish line, you will move to finish your course. You will have the strength, motivation, and desire to go all the way if you know your purpose. Get it settled, get it clear in your mind, set goals that you can work on today. And let the energy of knowing your destiny get and keep you going.

People with a Sense of Destiny Have Vital Relationships

No one can fulfill their destiny alone. We are part of the body of Christ and members one of another. Paul needed Barnabas, Silas, and Timothy. We all need others to fulfill the will of God. There are no "lone rangers" in the church, in business, or in the kingdom of God. (Even the Lone Ranger had Tonto.)

Proverbs 18:1 says, "A man who isolates himself . . . rages against all wise judgment." It seems that the greater the calling or destiny in one's life, the more one is inclined to think he or she can do it alone. I remember one minister telling the entire congregation that he didn't need them because he intended to do what God called him to do regardless of what they did. His arrogance and foolishness only alienated him from those he needed for support and for help with his vision of destiny. We all need each other.

Proverbs 11:14 tells us that "in the multitude of counselors there is safety." Before I make a major decision, I always consult the elders of our church and other pastors around the world who have become friends and partners through the years. Even when I'm sure I've heard from God, I want to test the word and let others judge it. If there is an error in my plan, others will see it and help me make changes before I get into trouble. If the plan is good they will confirm it and boost my confidence that it will work.

DESTINY KEY

NO ONE WILL FULFILL HIS OR HER DESTINY FROM GOD ALONE.

Those who "hear from God" and yet do not discuss their thoughts or plans with others are usually afraid of being wrong or too weak to face the challenge of counsel. They isolate themselves and act as though they are sure of everything they are doing while wondering on the inside if it will really work. Separation from others is a sign of insecurity and fear.

Relationships are God's way of bringing the gifts and talents we lack into our lives, ministries, and jobs. In Acts 15 we see how

important relationships were to Paul and Barnabas. The Lord had planned their destinies to flow together in a miraculous way. We also see that when relationships are broken it can throw us off our destiny course.

The two began their relationship when Barnabas went to Tarsus to seek Paul and bring him into the ministry in the church at Antioch. Barnabas was a great encourager and mentor and helped Paul develop his ministry and relationships with other Christian leaders. Soon they went on their first missionary trip together. In Acts 13:2, the Holy Spirit said to the group of prophets and teachers, "Now separate to Me Barnabas and Saul for the work to which I have called them."

Notice here that Barnabas was the leader of the team, and for the first years of their work together, he was the senior partner. But that changed, and soon we see them referred to as Paul and Barnabas. Paul had grown in his ministry and had risen to a place of greater influence and power. He and Barnabas started many churches together and went on more than one extended mission.

In Acts 15, they decided to go back to visit some of the brethren in various churches they had started. Barnabas wanted to take John Mark, who had gone with them on a previous trip but had become discouraged and turned back from the mission. Paul said, "No way." He was not interested in taking the young man with them (Acts 15:38). These two great men had such an argument over John Mark that the team was divided, and they went their separate ways.

Paul went on with Silas, and Barnabas went on to Cyprus with John Mark. From this point on, we never hear of Barnabas again. Paul and Silas start more churches and rise to great heights in ministerial effectiveness, but Barnabas is never mentioned again in terms of apostolic influence. Some speculate he had done his job with Paul, or that God divided them so they could multiply their labors, but I question that. These two mighty men could have split forces without going through contentions to do it. If the Holy Spirit had prompted the split, it would have been amicable, not the result of a bitter disagreement.

I believe that the breaking of the relationship threw Barnabas off his destiny course. I believe that Barnabas's apostolic influence was linked to Paul, and when he left Paul, he lost that influence. I'm

sure he did other great works and went on to be with the Lord. But in terms of influencing the then-known world and planting churches that would affect the world, Barnabas was finished when he broke his relationship with Paul. Paul went on to write two-thirds of the New Testament and have great influence throughout the world, but Barnabas was not heard from again.

> ***DESTINY KEY***
>
> GOD WILL ALWAYS PROVIDE THE PEOPLE AND RELATIONSHIPS WE NEED TO FULFILL OUR DESTINY.

The sad part is that Barnabas was right about John Mark. He did go on to be a powerful minister, and Paul even asked him for assistance at one point. John Mark wrote one of the Gospels and had a tremendous ministry, as Barnabas knew he would. But the mistake that Barnabas made was giving up a relationship connected with his destiny because of a disagreement. He should have told Paul, "I think you're wrong; you don't understand how to develop young ministers," had his say for the record, but then continued with Paul in the work they were doing. To destroy a relationship over a point of view is foolish. Team members often disagree, but we shouldn't end relationships over them.

Barnabas thwarted God's plan for him—he did not finish destiny's course—because he lost a key relationship. I have seen several people who lost out on some of their destiny, or on a marriage, children, or a ministry, because they walked away from key relationships. Stay with the people who have brought you to a place of destiny. Don't destroy relationships over disagreements. Remember, we are linked. No one is a lone ranger or a one-man show.

The last point I want you to see in this story is that God brought a substitute for Barnabas to carry on the work with Paul. Silas stepped in, and they went on as if nothing had happened. God will always provide the people and relationships we need to fulfill our destiny. In so doing, He provides them the opportunity to fulfill their own destiny course, as Silas did. When we have that sense of destiny in our life, we are like a magnet, drawing needed people to our efforts. They come ready to help with what the Lord has called them to do.

Steps to Your Destiny

Take time to meditate on the seven forces that flow from following destiny:

1. People with a sense of destiny have *vision*.
   What goals and purposes do you foresee for yourself in the upcoming month?

2. People with a sense of destiny have *discipline*.
   What bad habit or practice would you like to drop right away?

3. People with a sense of destiny have *self-esteem*.
   What recordings of inferiority are playing in your head?

4. People with a sense of destiny have *faith and courage*.
   What have you been afraid to pursue?

5. People with a sense of destiny have *resources*.
   Are you trusting God to meet all your needs?

6. People with a sense of destiny have *drive and motivation*.
   Do you get up each morning motivated to accomplish something?

7. People with a sense of destiny have vital *relationships*.
   Who in your life can you turn to for sound advice and counsel?

8

Staying on Destiny's Course

Getting on course with God's destiny for you will probably be easier for most of us than staying on course. I was reminded of this truth recently while bouncing through some rough air at 35,000 feet above the earth in a Boeing 747. The take-off is important, but it's the continued flight that gets you there!

Once we find our course of destiny in God and begin to move with Him to fulfill it, we must diligently stay the course. It is easy to get knocked off course like Barnabas did. There are so many ways it can happen. In the previous chapter we learned that Paul had much to say about perseverance when he spoke of friends in the ministry who had been spiritually shipwrecked before finishing their course. He said of himself, "But I discipline my body and bring it into subjection, lest, when I have preached to others, I myself should become disqualified" (1 Cor. 9:27). Paul's goal was not to lead the race for a few laps, but to be there at the finish line when it really counts. He said, "I press toward the goal" (Phil. 3:14).

The finish line is the goal. We must finish the course, arriving at the place where the Lord says, "Well done, good and faithful servant" (Matt. 25:21). We must not quit halfway, or be defeated before the ultimate victory, or get sidetracked into things that have nothing to do with our destiny. We must follow our course until it is finished.

In our world today, we find too many examples of people who start well but do not finish. There are people who never finish school, marriages that end in divorce, parents who don't take time to raise their own children, ministers that fall into sin and leave the ministry, churches that break up and close their doors. It is not enough to have a great beginning. We must play until the end of the game. We must go for all that God has planned for us. We must see the finish line and run to the end. Like Jesus, who said, "It is finished!" (John 19:30), and Paul, who said, "I have finished the race" (2 Tim. 4:7), you and I can complete our divine destinies.

There are seven enemies that have the potential to knock us off our course of destiny. Remember earlier I said that God has foreseen each of us and predestined us before the foundation of the world. In doing so, He crafted a perfect plan for your life and mine, a course of living that, if followed, will bring Him ultimate glory and will bring you and me complete joy and satisfaction. He gives us the choice of seeking out and following our destiny courses or settling for something less. Some of us will discover our course and begin down the path. That's when we need to know that there are enemies waiting to lead us astray. We need to be aware of them, so that we can finish God's destiny for our lives.

Let me say here that it is entirely possible that as you are on destiny's course and as you are actively fulfilling your destiny, you may make some mistakes and get temporarily knocked off course. But know that if you truly seek Him, God will give you the grace and the friends and the wisdom to get back on course again and finish fulfilling your destiny. Just cultivate a good heart and a sincere desire for God and His ways, and He will get you there. "He who has begun a good work in you will complete it until the day of Jesus Christ," Paul said (Phil. 1:6.).

Some enemies are obvious; others are subtle. But remember, when a plane is flying through the air, it doesn't take much of a course adjustment to make it veer in the wrong direction. One degree off course for a few hours of flight can put us in the wrong city, state, or even country. It may be little attitudes or decisions that cause the biggest detours on the way to our destiny. We must be alert and guard our lives and our destinies.

Seven Enemies That Can Knock You Off Course

1. Satan

To many, Satan is a myth, a figment of man's imagination, or a scapegoat created to take our blame. But to Jesus and to those who were God's instruments in writing the Bible, he is a real spiritual force who wants to destroy you (especially if you are on course with destiny). Peter said:

> *Be sober, be vigilant; because your adversary the devil walks about like a roaring lion, seeking whom he may devour. (1 Peter 5:8)*

Satan's major offensive is against your thought life. He is a master at placing thoughts in your mind in such a way that you become discouraged, fearful, confused, or deceived. He used thoughts to tempt Jesus in the wilderness and to try to convince Him to use His power for personal gain. Jesus was able to cast aside these thoughts and go on to His full destiny, but many Christians are not able to do likewise.

DESTINY KEY

THE GREATEST BATTLES ARE FOUGHT IN THE MIND.

Paul talked of thoughts that become strongholds in our lives (2 Cor. 10:4-5). Proverbs tells us that what we think controls who we are (Prov. 23:7). The greatest battles you and I fight are in the mind.

Satan and every other demon spirit can be controlled through the name of Jesus. We know this, and he knows this, so he must be careful not to show himself or we will quickly stop him.

> *"Behold, I give you the authority to trample on serpents and scorpions, and over all the power of the enemy, and nothing shall by any means hurt you." (Luke 10:19)*

> *"Assuredly, I say to you, whatever you bind on earth will be bound in heaven, and whatever you loose on earth will be loosed in heaven." (Matt. 18:18)*

> *At the name of Jesus every knee should bow, of those in heaven, and of those on earth, and of those under the earth, and . . . every tongue should confess that Jesus Christ is Lord, to the glory of God the Father. (Phil. 2:10-11)*

Subtlety and deception have been Satan's forte since the Garden of Eden, and they continue to be so today. When thoughts undermine, distract, discourage, and divide you from your destiny, you must take control.

First, say aloud, "In Jesus' name, I bind your influence, Satan, and the influence of every demonic spirit. I resist you, Satan, and you must flee. I focus on the Word of God and the thoughts of God. I submit to God. I am led by the Holy Spirit. No other spirit will influence my thoughts or life in any way."

Ephesians 4:27 warns not to "give place to the devil." If you do not give him a place to work in your life, he cannot do what he would like to do. You must guard your mind against Satan's influences, regardless of their source: other people, TV, movies, books, or anything that might sully your mind with sinful negativity. Satan can be defeated, but don't play games with him. Get serious! And get his influence out of your life!

2. Shortsightedness

Have you ever tried driving down the freeway while gazing about twenty feet in front of your car? I don't recommend this practice, but if you have ever done it, you probably discovered that it took about three lanes to stay on the freeway. Prolonging your shortsighted driving would have inevitably led to an accident. So it is with many families, churches, and businesses today. *Shortsightedness is causing many to weave and crash on their destiny course.*

How many TV interviews have we seen with a factory worker whining over the closure of his plant? We see the media condemning the corporation that ruined his family and caused such pain. We see the man crying about his lost job, the terrible economy, and the bleak future. The fact is, the worker probably knew for months what was coming. If he had read even a little bit of business news, he could have known what was in store for his company and his position. He was worrying about paying

the bills rather than discovering his destiny and developing a long-range plan for his life.

We may not know what tomorrow holds, but we know Who holds tomorrow. We can seek the Lord and pray for insights that will help us prepare for the future and the realization of our destiny.

> *Through wisdom a house is built,*
> *And by understanding it is established;*
> *By knowledge the rooms are filled*
> *With all precious and pleasant riches. (Prov. 24:3-4)*

The realization of one's destiny doesn't come in a moment, a month, or a year. It comes over a lifetime. You picked up this book, and you are gaining some revelation about your destiny. Next month perhaps you'll have realized a bit more of your destiny—covered some new ground, become more like Jesus, and accomplished new things for Him—by applying this book's principles and by traveling farther down destiny's course. It is a process, often slow, but sure.

DESTINY KEY

FULFILLMENT OF YOUR DESTINY DOES NOT COME IN A MOMENT, A MONTH, OR A YEAR, BUT OVER A LIFETIME.

To achieve a great destiny, we must be willing to look down the road of life, prepare for turns and bumps, and keep going no matter how long it takes or how tough it gets. Unfortunately, we have become an MTV generation, one that can rarely concentrate for more than three minutes at a time. We have lost the art of planning, envisioning, and enduring.

Every now and then, someone will impact your life in a significant way. This happened to me when I had the great fortune of meeting Peter Daniels. This Australian bricklayer was born again at twenty-six years of age and began a life of destiny, one that lifted him to a higher level and enabled him to help thousands of others to rise to a higher level as well.

Peter's number-one message is what he calls *Life Goals*. In it, he asks:

"What can you accomplish over the years of your life if you commit yourself completely and give everything you have to the fulfillment of that goal?"

What can I live for, work for, give for, serve for, and die for? What goal will make full use of my gifts, abilities, and energies? What will hold my attention and excitement until I die?

To what cause would you give yourself for a lifetime? That is my question to you today. Stop thinking about this month, this year, and this decade for a moment. What will you do for the *rest of your life* that will result in God saying to you, "Well done, good and faithful servant"? It may take you months to answer that question, and you may change your answer along the way. But the point is that we are thinking in terms of a lifetime, not just short-term. Eventually we'll move into thinking about generations and legacies, but for now we'll work on lifetime goals.

No matter what it takes, get yourself thinking long-term. Start writing things down. Start searching your heart and the opportunities around you. Don't be just a "flash in the pan" of life. Be a diamond of enduring value and taste. Don't be shortsighted.

The fact is, we must be patient with ourselves and understand that fruit grows in stages, not all at once. Everything in the kingdom of God works on the seed principle.

> *And He said, "The kingdom of God is as if a man should scatter seed on the ground, and should sleep by night and rise by day, and the seed should sprout and grow, he himself does not know how. For the earth yields crops by itself: first the blade, then the head, after that the full grain in the head. But when the grain ripens, immediately he puts in the sickle, because the harvest has come. (Mark 4:26-29)*

I wish the seed would sprout and grow immediately, but it doesn't. Notice in the parable that the farmer must sleep and rise. Who knows how many nights and days he'll sleep and rise before the seed has grown? He must be patient and let the crop grow at its own pace. No matter what he does, he cannot speed up the process. Though I know this is true, I still want to make things

happen faster. I keep checking the plant to see if it's time for harvest. I do it so often that I sometimes disturb the plant and actually hinder its growth.

Growth doesn't happen overnight unless it is in some way abnormal or mutated. In nature we can induce super growth, but the plant is usually a freak and has inbred problems that cause early death. So it is in ministry or business. We may be able to promote rapid growth and make things happen quickly, but it usually brings other problems that destroy the fruit down the road. The best way to have an abundant harvest is to plant the seed, sleep and rise, and let the growth happen naturally.

> *For you have need of endurance, so that after you have done the will of God, you may receive the promise:*
> *"For yet a little while,*
> *And He who is coming will come and will not tarry.*
> *Now the just shall live by faith;*
> *But if anyone draws back,*
> *My soul has no pleasure in him."* (Heb. 10:36-38)

It is possible that you have done the will of God—that you have kept on destiny's course—though you have not yet seen the results. You may be wondering, "What's wrong?" It's possible that nothing is wrong and that you need to go to bed (figuratively speaking) and let the seed grow. You have done the will of God, now relax. Don't think that everything must happen at once. It's not easy to wait for things to grow. We admire the guy who made his first million by the time he was twenty-five. We pick up lunch at the drive-through window, and we cook dinner in the microwave. The mentality of our society is, "Why wait?" "Why wait until we're married? Let's have sex now." "Why work out the marriage problems? Let's get divorced and try someone else."

It goes against our flesh to be patient. But it sure helps in fulfilling one's destiny. Much of what God calls us to occupationally is a matter of timing. Though you know God wants you to start a church or business, the big questions in your mind should be, "When and where?" That's why James says we need to ask God for wisdom. Knowledge tells you what God wants you to

do, then wisdom tells you when, where, and how. Wisdom tells you not to be thrown off course by shortsightedness and impatience, but to work over the long haul to achieve your full destiny.

3. Unhealthy Desires

Desires can be powerful. When used for God, they direct us to our destiny. When used for the flesh or the world, they distract us and divide our energies. In T. L. Osborn's book *The Positive Power of Desires*, I learned that God did not want to destroy my desires and turn me into some kind of "empty blob." In fact, God *gives* me desires and uses them to motivate me to do His will. One of the ways man is like God is his ability to have desires. We must discipline ourselves to keep our desires focused on those things that will move us toward our destiny and away from those things that will not.

> *Delight yourself also in the LORD,*
> *And He shall give you the desires of your heart.* (Ps. 37:4)

This verse contains two truths. First, if we will delight in the Lord, He will place desires in us. These have to do with our destiny. There is a reason you like the things you like and have a desire to do the things you do. I look at some people and wonder why they desire to do what they are doing. I would never want to do that. But you see, God has not put that desire in me because it's unrelated to my destiny. What you desire is often a sign of your calling.

The second truth is that when I am delighted in the Lord and not in the flesh, God is pleased to grant my desires, which are now in accordance with His will. The Lord takes pleasure in the prosperity of His people, both in their ministries and in their personal lives. I have experienced this truth.

During a New Year holiday, one of our church members took me out to lunch. As we sat talking about family and business, he presented me with the title to a beautiful Harley Davidson Sportster 1200, something I had long desired. I had never talked about this desire publicly, but God knew about it. God is so good to His children.

Because desires are so powerful, we must be careful which ones we allow to grow. Desires can be fed and developed like our appetite. At first no one enjoys smoking cigarettes, but the more you do it, the stronger your desire becomes, until the desire to smoke becomes a part of you. No one likes the taste of alcohol when they first try it, but you develop the desire for it as you continue to drink. Watching soap operas is not a natural habit or desire; it is developed by watching them until they become a part of your life.

People become addicted to pornography and perverted sex by feeding these unnatural desires. Once a desire takes root and becomes a habit or a part of their life, they feel they can no longer control it—they are trapped.

The same thing happens in adultery or fornication. The desire for a woman or man starts as a passing thought. But as it becomes your focus and you fantasize about that person and what the two of you could do together, the desire begins to grow. Over time that desire gets stronger, until you begin to plan ways to make it happen. Then the desire ultimately overwhelms you, and you find yourself in sin. Many a great destiny has been thwarted because of a desire for the wrong things. We must not let our desires control our lives. *We must discipline ourselves!*

DESTINY KEY

DESIRES CAN BE FED AND DEVELOPED LIKE OUR APPETITE.

Healthy desires—the desire to reach more people with the Word of God, to build more facilities for ministry or business, or to make more money so you can give more and can better care for your family—are equally powerful. Focus your thoughts on the positive things you can attain in your life and career. If it's within God's destiny and plan for you, go for it. Don't be nervous about doing something wrong. God will direct your heart. Paul tried to go to the wrong place several times, but God redirected him to the right place. Allow your God-given desires to grow and be a motivational force in your life. Just make sure you keep your desires in line with your destiny. Inappropriate desires can shipwreck you.

4. Deceit of Money

"The love of money is a root of all kinds of evil" (1 Tim. 6:10). Both Jesus and Paul warned us how tricky money can be. We need money to do what God has called us to do. God wants you to have money and to prosper. But He does not want the money to have you. That's where the rich young ruler (Mark 10:17-22) missed it. The Lord wanted to give him abundant life in return for his possessions. But because the ruler's possessions owned him, he could not let them go. The young man missed the greatest opportunity he could ever have had. It's hard for a rich man to enter into heaven when his wealth is his god.

Paul said it is "the love of money" that causes all evil. It controls the decisions, actions, and lifestyles of most Americans. Rather than trusting in God and obeying His Word, our society trusts in money and will do whatever it takes to get more. The inscription on our currency should be changed from "In God We Trust" to "In Money We Trust."

When ministries start doing things just to make more money, or when we compromise our ethics and integrity to raise money, we are on a downward slide that will cost us greatly. It's tempting, and none of us are exempt. I know how it feels when the bills are piling up and an opportunity to make money comes along. There is a strong temptation to do whatever it takes to get the money. You begin to focus on your need rather than on the Word and will of God. We must fight that temptation.

God is our source, and when we keep ourselves right with Him, He will meet all our needs according to His riches in glory. When we start doing it our way, we will always lose.

The best way to guard against the deceitfulness of money is to be a generous giver. Start by giving your tithe; then see how much more of your income you can give away.

5. Stress

"Be strong and of good courage" (Deut. 31:6). No doubt about it, there will be some stress along the way to fulfilling your destiny. Stress is a useful thing if you handle it correctly. Stressing the muscles makes them stronger and your body healthier—*if* you are exercising and stressing muscles in the right way.

The same is true emotionally, mentally, and spiritually. We must stretch ourselves if we want to progress and to fulfill our destiny. That means we will go through some stress. Life with no stress would be boring, unfulfilling, and empty. The key is having the right *kind* of stress and managing it in the right way.

The following forms of stress can be good if we react in a positive way:

- *Career or job challenges that enable us to acquire new abilities and greater wisdom.* Acquiring new job skills and increasing our responsibilities often leads to increased self-esteem and improved income.
- *Relationship problems that motivate us to sit down and talk with a loved one or friend in a way that we never have before, or to discuss matters we've avoided in the past.* Any time pain drives us to seek a deeper, healthier understanding of each other, the stress has been positive and the results will be worthwhile.
- *Weight or health problems that cause us to change our diet and begin to exercise, so that we will live longer and healthier lives.* Some folks literally eat themselves to death with too much food or the wrong kinds of food. Obesity, stomach problems, or heart problems are often a wake-up call. If we respond positively, we have a chance for a new body, a new lifestyle, and a new lease on life.

The negative results of stress come when we begin to internalize the fear, worry, and anxiety that problems can bring. Lying awake at night and worrying about the bills, the job, our weight, or our relationships will add to our troubles. Now we not only have the trouble, but we have the symptoms that the stress over the trouble can bring.

DESTINY KEY

STRESS CAN BE A USEFUL THING IF YOU HANDLE IT RIGHT.

The worst part about negative stress is that it can choke the Word of God in our lives. Mark 4:19 says, "And the cares of this world . . . choke the word, and

it becomes unfruitful." That means that you stop receiving the strength and the answers that God's Word provides because you are caught up in fear and anxiety. That can soon drain you, and you can be defeated by the problem rather than defeating it with the Word.

Paul said in 2 Timothy 1:7, "For God has not given us a spirit of fear, but of power and of love and of a sound mind." The spirit of fear is what keeps you focused on the bad things that could happen, the things that may go wrong, and reasons the future looks bleak. It weakens and drains you until you are hemmed in by the circumstances of life and cannot find a way out. You have fallen down and can't get up.

If you know much about David's life, you know he faced more stress than most of us ever will. When he returned to his city and found that it had been destroyed by fire (1 Sam. 30) and that all the women and children had been taken captive by the enemy, David overcame worry and stress and stayed on destiny's course by following a proactive course.

David confessed his anguish openly. He did not try to internalize his feelings and act as though he had everything under control. That's often where illness comes from. Confession of our feelings releases them and allows us to change and move on.

David encouraged himself in the Lord. He began to recall the words that God had given to him. He may have spent some time singing and worshiping the Lord. He meditated on the Scripture and God's promises to His people. Soon David was ready to take charge of his circumstances, not just be victimized by them.

David inquired of the Lord and got an answer. He prayed, but not just to hear himself pray. He prayed for guidance. Under pressure, many people pray, not seeking God's answers but releasing emotional pressure. This is okay, but we also need to seek answers from God. The Lord will direct our steps if we turn to Him for answers.

David pursued his enemy with a vision of recovering all he'd lost. He wasn't sitting around crying about the big, bad Amalekites. David was going to attack and recover it all. There must be a point of action for all of us—a time we quit complaining and start doing something. Wallowing in our anger and grief doesn't change anything.

David defeated his enemy. He fought until the enemy was wiped out. Your enemy may be weight or a negative outlook or financial lack—whatever is causing you unhealthy stress and worry. Fight it, defeat it, and turn it around. Jesus said, "The kingdom of heaven suffers violence, and the violent take it by force" (Matt. 11:12).

David recovered what he had lost. Don't stop until you have reached your goal and eradicated the sources of stress and worry from your life. You can do it. You can make it. The better job is there. The healed marriage is waiting for you. The healthier body can be yours. The friendship you're looking for is just around the corner. But you must persist till you achieve your goal. So many people start and then hesitate; they give up just when they're about to make it. Don't stop until you succeed! Get everything God has for you!

6. Ego and Pride

"Pride goes before destruction, and a haughty spirit before a fall" (Prov. 16:18). Man's ego is a funny thing. It can make us think we are more than we really are, but it can also cause us to think we are less. I've seen so many people try to be something they are not, try to achieve a destiny that was not theirs, and then when failure and destruction come, they end up living beneath themselves and the wonderful destiny that God had for them. Some never get started on their destiny course, because they cannot humble themselves to learn, grow, and change.

> ***DESTINY KEY***
>
> SOME NEVER GET STARTED ON THEIR DESTINY COURSE BECAUSE THEY CANNOT HUMBLE THEMSELVES TO LEARN, GROW, AND CHANGE.

When we begin to think we're cool, when we pridefully think, "Man, look at me; I've got this destiny thing down!"—we're on our way to a fall. Anything that works in our life is working because *God* has willed it to be, allowed it to be. When we regard it as a personal accomplishment, pride sets in. Pride causes us to let down our guard and open the door for the attacks

of Satan through sin, compromise, foolishness, or harmful relationships.

Satan's greatest sin was to believe he was to have God's glory. He thought the angelic beings of heaven should worship *him*. He thought *he* should be the object of the praise, worship, and glory all around him. When he began to be full of pride and exalt himself, he lost his relationship with God, entered into sin and rebellion, and ended up being kicked out of heaven. Pride can make us think crazy things about ourselves and our circumstances. It can also get us kicked out of the presence of God.

> ***DESTINY KEY***
>
> GOD IS FORGIVING AND MERCIFUL, AND HIS DESTINY FOR US IS RESILIENT AND STRONG.

The other thing that pride does is stop us from openly repenting when we are wrong. Mistakes are not usually a fatal blow to our destiny. God is forgiving and merciful, and His destiny for us is resilient and strong. But unconfessed, unrepented sin will kill us and destroy our destiny. Pride tells us to keep the image up and act as though everything is cool, but if we fail to confess our sins, our lives start to fall apart. By not repenting openly, we give sin power to rise again.

Man's ego is one of the wonders of the world. It is powerful enough to move us through wars and battles of every kind, yet it is so weak that one person can crush it—especially when that person is our spouse. Peter Daniels says, "A wife holds the ego of her husband in the palm of her hand."

I've seen it in my own life. After preaching a message that leads to many being born again, the first thing I say when I see Wendy is, "What did you think?" I want affirmation that I did great!

We must not let pride or ego control our decisions or actions in any way. Learn to recognize the feelings of pride or egotistical motivation and stop them. Pride is a manifestation of the weakness of our flesh. If we let this weakness control our decisions, we will eventually fail. We will lose our destiny's bearings.

Many ministers are so egotistical that they cannot be challenged or confronted. They guard their ego and their pride by avoiding discussion of any issues that may demand change on their part. This will eventually catch up with them and destroy them. They won't be able to see their destiny. They'll be too busy looking at themselves.

I remember one leader saying he had no one to talk to about problems in his life. The fact is, he acted like he had no problems and if anyone challenged anything in his life or ministry, he would avoid them or fire them. If we deny our flesh, set aside our pride, and sanctify our ego, we're not showing weakness but rather strength. By being open to constructive criticism, we show we are not defensive, and others will have more respect for us.

One example of this in our own ministry is with the local media of Seattle. Every time they call concerning some religious story they want to do or even some negative story they are trying to do about Christian Faith Center, I am quick to respond and meet with them. I have nothing to hide. I don't try to avoid them, and I don't respond defensively to their questioning.

While doing a local show for CBS, one of the reporters reminded me of a story he had done on our church several years ago. He recalled how impressed he was that we were accessible, open, and not afraid to be challenged. The story came out well, and we have built as good a relationship with the secular media as can be expected.

Don't let your ego or pride cause you to do things, or keep you from doing things. You are never too big to serve or be challenged. If you are really going strong in your calling and destiny, the questions or comments of others will not hurt you. Only the weak will avoid, deny, hide, and react.

7. Fear

Paul said that "God has not given us a spirit of fear" (2 Tim. 1:7). Some folks never get going with their destiny because the spirit of fear grips their life. There are three major areas of fear that stop or hinder the pursuit of destiny in many:

Fear of change. This is a big one in the religious world. So many don't want change. Even if what they are doing doesn't work, they keep on doing it. They would rather ride a dead horse than get off and climb on a fresh one. Change is the way of life. Anything that lives and grows constantly changes. We must become good at adapting.

Especially in today's world of technological and social change, we must be ready and willing to go through a constant evolution. We must make adjustments and be flexible enough to handle whatever circumstances come our way. In marriage there is a continual demand to change. As Wendy and I grow older, as our children grow older, and as our ministry and careers grow, we must change the way we think, communicate, and act. Life is in a constant state of flux.

DESTINY KEY

CHANGE IS A NORMAL PROCESS OF LIFE, AND THE BETTER YOU HANDLE IT, THE MORE GOD WILL USE YOU.

When my Grandmother Roxie passed on to be with the Lord at age eighty-six, I thought about the life she and my Grandfather Mac had lived. As children they traveled on horses and coal-driven trains. Later they saw the development of the car and began to drive. Finally they began to fly in jet airplanes around the world. Their generation's lifestyle changed more radically than any in human history to date. Change has become a way of life.

We must be comfortable with change, accept it, and learn to use it to our advantage. To some, even a change in hair style is a dramatic event! It shouldn't be. Change is a normal process of life, and the better you handle it, the more God can use you. Don't hang on to traditions that mean nothing in terms of biblical truth. Don't rail against new styles, contemporary thoughts, or new ideas that come into the world (if they seem to be of God). Flow with the tides of change. Ride the crests to your destiny.

Fear of failure. This fear has paralyzed many. The fear of failure causes you to be overly careful, overly cautious, to avoid step-

ping out. I never ran for a leadership office in school because I was afraid to lose. I probably would have been a good student officer, but I will never know because I was afraid of failure. How many things might you be good at but you'll never know because you will not try?

When Jesus called to the disciples as He was walking on the water (Matt. 14:25-33), Peter was the only one to get out of the boat. There was a chance that Peter would get his robe wet on the bottom (and he did), but there was also a chance that he would walk with Jesus on the water—and he did! The other eleven disciples remained in the boat because they were afraid they might sink. They didn't sink, but they also never walked on water! Only Peter did that. Fear of failure will keep you in the boat. It will stop you from trusting God and moving on in your destiny.

I've seen so many called to the ministry who never started because they didn't know where they were going to get the money. They wanted to have a guaranteed salary, an insurance package, and a retirement program before they would start. But God says, "If you want to do My will, then let's go! Take My hand, and let's get on with your destiny."

There will be things we do that don't work. I've lost count of the projects, services, and ideas that have failed during my fifteen years of ministry. But none of those failures have stopped me from continuing to grow and fulfill my destiny. In fact, they have helped me to learn, to grow, to better understand my destiny. The one thing that can stop us from fulfilling our destiny is to stop moving. If we don't try, we will be finished. A paralyzing fear of failure is much more damaging to the achievement of destiny than failure itself. We can always call out to Jesus if we begin to sink. The Lord lifted Peter to the top of the water, and the two walked to the boat together. You may begin to sink now and then, but Jesus will be there. He's closer to you when you are stepping out in faith than when you are sitting back in fear.

Fear of success. This fear is a little more subtle but just as damaging as the fear of failure. Many people have been programmed with negative thoughts and attitudes. Because of parents who instilled a negative mentality, teachers who taught

secular humanism, or churches that dwell on condemnation, many people fear success. They actually think it is *bad* to do too well. They are programmed to be average. To rise to the top of their field, to prosper financially, or to accomplish something great would overwhelm them, so they avoid it.

Fear of success causes some people to sabotage their own lives. Life begins to go too smoothly, so they do something to mess it up. I had a friend who was getting his degree in college, working in the field of his choice, and raising a great family. But one day he walked in and quit school and his job. He struggled for months to get back on course with his destiny. As we talked about why he did what he did, he realized that his actions were motivated by a fear of success. He had sabotaged his life because he was doing better than everyone else in his family. He was living a life they had said he could never live. He had gone beyond the limiting thoughts of his upbringing, so he felt inwardly motivated to mess it up and get back to what was comfortable and "normal" for him and his family. Even if the old ways were a bummer, they were comfortable. Habits and lifestyles are like an old pair of shoes. They may be ugly, worn out, and falling apart, but at least they're comfortable.

Many commit adultery, quit their job, or get sick when things are going too well. Their subconscious minds are programmed for failure. If their salary or their spirit rises too high, they must bring it down a few notches. We must conquer our fear of success with thoughts that are focused on God's desire for us to have abundant success—in all areas of our lives.

DESTINY KEY

KEEP YOUR MIND FREE OF THE FEARS AND WORRIES OF LIFE.

Are you more important than a bird or a flower? That's the question Jesus asked his disciples as he taught them about worry and anxiety. He said, "Do not worry about tomorrow, for tomorrow will worry about its own things. Sufficient for the day is its own trouble" (Matt. 6:34). If God loves and cares for the birds and the flowers (who never worry about their future), how much more will He care for you?

Our world has become consumed with worry, partly because of the barrage of bad news with which we're confronted every day (some of it contrived to elevate media ratings). Alcohol, drugs, TV, and sports are important to us because they take our minds off the things we are worried about. We seek distractions. We don't want to think about the world's problems. Yet every morning they are back in our face, and we worry about them again. Rather than trying to avoid facing the issues of life, we should change the way we think about them. We shouldn't need to have a drink, smoke a joint, or watch a game to get our minds off the cares of this world.

If we looked at each issue in our world from a biblical perspective, we would know that God has everything under control. If we will trust Him, He will take care of us. If we try to solve our problems ourselves, God's provision won't flow as well. Peter tells us in 1 Peter 5:7 to cast "all your care upon Him, for He cares for you." He cannot help us if we cling to our problems and stubbornly insist on solving them ourselves. But He can and will solve the problems we release to Him.

Proverbs 3:5 says, "Trust in the LORD with all your heart, and lean not on your own understanding." If we try to figure everything out and handle it ourselves, we will be anxious and confused. The world is full of people living on tranquilizers and antacids while trying to work out their own problems. God will direct our paths and give us victory if we will only allow Him to. Let the peace of God that passes understanding keep your hearts and minds through Christ Jesus (Phil. 4:7). Your mind can never sort out all of the issues of life, so let God handle them.

Keep your mind clear from fear. Your worry or anxiety can't make one thing better anyway. All it does is hinder your faith and destroy your health. Let God handle your problems. Let Him sort out the issues of your life. "You will keep him in perfect peace, whose mind is stayed on You, because he trusts in You" (Isa. 26:3).

Steps to Your Destiny

Here are seven enemies that could knock you off destiny's course:

1. *Satan.* What thoughts has Satan placed in your mind that you should release?

2. *Shortsightedness.* In what areas of life do you need a long-term vision?

3. *Unhealthy desires.* What are your desires? Give them to God and let Him sanctify them for His use!

4. *Deceit of money.* In what one area of your life could you sacrifice spending on yourself and instead give to God?

5. *Stress.* In what areas are you experiencing stress in your life? How can you turn this stress into a creative, positive experience?

6. *Ego and pride.* In what areas are they potential problems? Your looks? Your work? Your parenting? Give your ego to God and allow Him to use it to open new doors for growth.

7. *Fear.* What are you afraid of? Change? Failure? Success? What fear is holding you back from God's best for your life?

9

Using Your Faith

Have you ever heard someone say, "If God wants it to happen, it will happen"? This is a way of saying "God is responsible for everything that goes on in my life, and I have nothing to do with it." By now you know that is not what I teach. In fact, it is our responsibility to discern and act on our destiny. God has set it forth for us, but we must seek and follow it.

In this chapter, we will discuss a key ingredient in discovering and living out our destiny: faith. "Without faith it is impossible to please Him" (Heb. 11:6), and so we can deduce that without faith, it is impossible to live out our destiny. Everything you have learned in the previous chapters matters little unless you bring it to life with faith. The knowledge is the car; faith is the gasoline. You may have read all of these chapters, and you may have put together a beautiful car by now, but you're not going to get anywhere in pursuit of your destiny without God's gas—faith.

Faith is:

- A lifestyle
  The just shall live by faith. (Rom. 1:17)

- An attitude
  And Peter answered Him and said, "Lord, if it is You,

command me to come to You on the water." So He said, "Come." And when Peter had come down out of the boat, he walked on the water to go to Jesus. (Matt. 14:28-29)

- A confession

  "For assuredly, I say to you, whoever says to this mountain, 'Be removed and be cast into the sea,' and does not doubt in his heart, but believes that those things he says will be done, he will have whatever he says." (Mark 11:23)

- A creative power

  Now faith is the substance of things hoped for, the evidence of things not seen. For by it the elders obtained a good testimony. By faith we understand that the worlds were framed by the word of God, so that the things which are seen were not made of things which are visible. (Heb. 11:1-3)

- An act of worship

  But without faith it is impossible to please Him, for he who comes to God must believe that He is, and that He is a rewarder of those who diligently seek Him. (Heb. 11:6)

- A seed that grows

  "Assuredly, I say to you, if you have faith as a mustard seed, you will say to this mountain, 'Move from here to there,' and it will move; and nothing will be impossible for you." (Matt. 17:20)

- A gift of the Spirit

  For I say, through the grace given to me, to everyone who is among you, not to think of himself more highly than he ought to think, but to think soberly, as God has dealt to each one a measure of faith. (Rom. 12:3)

  But the manifestation of the Spirit is given to each one for the profit of all . . . to another faith by the same Spirit. (1 Cor. 12:7, 9)

Our relationship with God begins with faith, and it is faith that carries us along with Him through every circumstance. If we do not exercise faith, God will allow us to live without Him, die without Him, and exist without Him for eternity. God will never force His destiny plan on us. We must open our life to Him and receive His will and plan through faith. Think of all the things that happen because of faith:

- We are saved by faith.
  If you confess with your mouth the Lord Jesus and believe in your heart that God has raised Him from the dead, you will be saved. For with the heart one believes unto righteousness, and with the mouth confession is made unto salvation. (Rom. 10:9-10)

- We live by faith.
  For in it the righteousness of God is revealed from faith to faith; as it is written, "The just shall live by faith." (Rom. 1:17)

  That no one is justified by the law in the sight of God is evident, for "the just shall live by faith." (Gal. 3:11)

  Now the just shall live by faith;
  But if anyone draws back,
  My soul has no pleasure in him. (Heb. 10:38)

- We pray the prayer of faith.
  And the prayer of faith will save the sick, and the Lord will raise him up. (James 5:15)

- We fight the fight of faith.
  Fight the good fight of faith, lay hold on eternal life, to which you were also called and have confessed the good confession in the presence of many witnesses. (1 Tim. 6:12)

- We keep the faith.
  I have fought the good fight, I have finished the race, I have kept the faith. (2 Tim. 4:7)

- We walk by faith.
  For we walk by faith, not by sight. (2 Cor. 5:7)
- We speak the Word of faith.
  "The word is near you, in your mouth and in your heart" (that is, the word of faith which we preach). (Rom. 10:8)

- We please God with faith.
  But without faith it is impossible to please Him, for he who comes to God must believe that He is, and that He is a rewarder of those who diligently seek Him. (Heb. 11:6)

- We receive a good testimony by faith.
  For by it [faith] the elders obtained a good testimony. (Heb. 11:2)

- We take up the shield of faith.
  Above all, taking the shield of faith with which you will be able to quench all the fiery darts of the wicked one. (Eph. 6:16)

- We take the kingdom by faith.
  And from the days of John the Baptist until now the kingdom of heaven suffers violence, and the violent take it by force. (Matt. 11:12)

Faith is the substance of all the things you have been hoping for. When you add faith to hope, those things will begin to manifest in your life. Of course, you realize that Jesus is talking about godly things that are within the realm of your destiny. You can't have faith for something that is contrary to the plan of God for your life and expect it to come to pass.

Many have tried to use faith to start a church, or to be an evangelist, or to launch a business, or to initiate a relationship, but it wasn't within their destiny. It was a personal desire, so it never came to pass. That is why we have said so much about destiny before we got to the subject of faith. When you know your destiny, you can exercise your faith and see great things come to pass.

Having Faith That Moves Mountains

Faith is so basic to the things of God that it is amazing how many Christians have never been taught its principles. The New Testament is full of commands and instructions on faith. Jesus commands us to "have faith in God" (Mark 11:22). He then tells us how to use that faith to move the mountains in our life. With faith we can overcome the obstacles on our destiny course. We can't just sit back and have faith that our destiny will happen. We must actively seek our destiny. How? By acting on our faith.

Many people believe that faith is just believing in something, but James says that even Satan believes. James 2:20 says "faith without works is dead." In other words, action must correspond to your faith. Faith is not something we *have* as much as it is something we *do*. It is an action verb that causes us to speak and to do things that produce supernatural results. Just saying we believe in God will not get us saved or into heaven. Satan believes in God. Everyone in hell believes in God. To have faith in God means that we will confess with our mouth that Jesus is Lord and believe in our heart that God raised Him from the dead (Rom. 10:9-10).

Faith in God means that you will speak to the mountains in your life and command them to move, not just call your friend and talk about the mountains! The world talks *about* its problems, but faith-filled people talk *to* them. Jesus spoke to trees, storms, mountains, sickness, and demons to show us how to use our faith. He showed us by example that if we say with our mouth and believe with our heart that God-glorifying things will happen, they will, because God honors faith. Faith is not just believing that God is; it is obeying God, speaking His Word, and believing that God will change our circumstances.

In the course of your destiny, Satan will always try to challenge your faith. He will come against you through people who are evil or just unaware of truth. He will use circumstances to deceive and distract you. He will try to stop you from being all that God destined you to be. It's up to you to keep the faith, to walk by faith and not by sight, to fight the good fight, to speak to the storm, and to walk on the water. If you sit back and wait for God

to make everything easy, you will accomplish nothing. If you think pursuing your destiny will be a journey of ease, you are mistaken. It will be fun, fulfilling, and rewarding, but it will be a battle to the end. It will be a good battle because God has guaranteed us victory if we will follow His plan.

You will meet resistance. The enemy will come at you in different ways, and you must decide to fight no matter what he throws at you. Christians must have a fighting spirit and the willingness to take God's destiny by force. This attitude is so different from the one that is traditionally portrayed as "Christian." We cannot be spineless worms and expect to fulfill the destiny of God. Like Paul, we must fight the fight of faith, take the kingdom by force, and have a courageous spirit. Only then will we overcome our enemies.

The Fight of Faith

If you are on course with your destiny but do not understand or use the principle of faith, you could hinder your destiny. We see this in the story of Israel. It was God's plan for them to possess the Promised Land, but because of their unbelief, many died in the wilderness. They lacked the faith to persevere to the end. Later, after Joshua led them into the Promised Land, they never possessed all that God said they could, again because they became slack and lost their faith (Josh. 18:1-3).

DESTINY KEY

THE FAITH-FILLED LIFE IS DIFFICULT BECAUSE IT FORCES US TO CONTROL OUR THOUGHTS AND DISCIPLINE OUR BODIES.

A great number of Christians will die in the wilderness of life or will die never having possessed all that God has made available to them. They will go to heaven, but they won't fulfill their destiny on the earth because they don't walk by faith. The faith-filled life is difficult in many ways because it forces us to control our thoughts and discipline our bodies. We must keep our eyes focused on Jesus

and His Word, not on the circumstances around us. "For we walk by faith, not by sight" (2 Cor. 5:7). That means that what we know from God's Word must become more real to us than what we know by our natural senses.

I've never seen the Lamb's Book of Life, but I believe it is real, and I believe my name is written in it. When secular humanists deny the presence of God or the reality of heaven, it is because they live by sight (natural senses) not by faith. They do not accept anything that their human senses cannot confirm. Therefore they have no relationship with God.

In the same way, many Christians deny certain parts of the Scripture because they cannot understand them. Though they believe in God, they do not believe in certain works of the Holy Spirit, in God's healing power, or in His ability to answer prayer. They too walk by sight, not by faith. This limits what the Lord can do in their lives, and though they are saved, they may not fulfill their destiny.

Even the apostle Paul, who had such a great destiny in the Lord, had to fight the fight of faith to make it to his destiny's end. There were many times when he could have said, "Well, if God wants it to happen it will happen." But he didn't. He used his faith to overcome his circumstances and get on with his destiny. When the religious people of the day tried to stop him, he believed God would give him the strength to overcome them. When evil men attacked him, he believed God would deliver him. When storms wrecked his ship, he believed God would save him. When he ran out of money, he believed God would meet his needs. When he felt weak, he believed God's power was still working in him, and he went on by faith.

Paul never said, "If it is God's will, it will happen." He *fought* to fulfill God's will. He prayed; he believed; he stood on the Word of God and never gave in to his circumstances or natural feelings.

Today, we often let the storms of life decide our direction. We let our circumstances dictate our behavior. Fight the fight of faith! Use faith in God to move mountains, to calm the storms, and to overcome problems.

Faith: It's More Than a Nice Thought

How did Paul do it? How did he overcome adversity and still fight the fight of faith? Paul said in 2 Corinthians 4:8:

> *We are hard pressed on every side, yet not crushed; we are perplexed, but not in despair; persecuted, but not forsaken; struck down, but not destroyed.*

I like to say that Paul was struck down but not struck out! How did Paul handle his problems? How did he overcome? Verse 13 tells us:

> *Since we have the same spirit of faith, according to what is written, "I believed and therefore I spoke," we also believe and therefore speak.*

So you want to be like Paul. You want to live the Christian life and fight the fight of faith. There seem to be many people in that camp, yet few rise to live their destiny. Why? *They do not have the spirit of faith.* The spirit of faith kept Paul going, not the things he felt or experienced or saw in the natural realm. The spirit of faith caused him to speak.

The spirit of faith caused Paul to keep his eyes on the things that aren't seen, for the things that are seen are temporary (2 Cor. 4:18).

Faith involves choice. We choose to believe the Word of God and to trust God in every situation, or we choose to look at the circumstances and believe what we see. We walk by faith, or we walk by sight. Paul chose to walk by faith no matter what came against him, and that is how he fulfilled his destiny. It happened because Paul used his faith in accordance with the plan of God.

To Paul, faith was more than just a nice thought. Many people know about the doctrine of faith. They have heard sermons on faith. They can even quote Scriptures about faith. But they don't *have* the spirit of faith. Paul said it was the spirit of faith that kept him in pursuit of his destiny. Faith is more than a quaint Christian belief. It is a part of your being—a part of your spirit and soul. It is an attitude, a way of thinking. It is a way of life!

I know people who have come from so-called "faith schools" and have been involved with so-called "faith ministries" but have never had the spirit of faith. They have heard great sermons on faith and a good doctrine of faith. They even have spoken the word of faith, but it wasn't really part of them. The results of faith were not there. Their ministry, church, or business never manifested the fruit of faith because they did not operate in God's plan.

The spirit of faith causes us to walk with love, power, and a sound mind (2 Tim. 1:7), never with a spirit of fear. So many people today worry about their money, their safety, their reputation, their children, and their future because they do not have a spirit of faith. God did not give them a spirit of fear; they picked it up from the world. They walk by sight rather than by faith.

In Numbers 14 the Israelites believed the ten spies who gave a bad report and decided that they would not go into the Promised Land. (The majority is usually wrong.) They cried all night and talked of killing Moses and electing a new leader to take them back to Egypt. As with many Christians today, when challenged with storms, "giants," and difficult situations, instead of walking by faith they were consumed with fear. They were ready to turn back from their destiny course. (We must remember that our destiny will not be fulfilled just because it is God's design. We must walk by faith!) But while Israel cried and mourned, Moses interceded for them. Then God said that those who were twenty years of age and older would die in the wilderness because of their unbelief—with two exceptions: Joshua and Caleb, who had given a faith-filled report when they came back from spying out the land. They walked by faith and not by sight. God said they would go into the Promised Land and fulfill their destiny, while every other adult would die young.

In Numbers 14:24, notice what the Lord said about Caleb:

> *But My servant Caleb, because he has a different spirit in him and has followed Me fully, I will bring into the land where he went, and his descendants shall inherit it.*

God fulfilled His will for Caleb and his family because Caleb had a different spirit, a spirit of faith. To fulfill our destinies, we

must have a different spirit from the world around us. We must have a spirit that causes us to see that the land of milk and honey is ours. We need a spirit that says, "I can do it!" when everyone else says, "There's no way." That is the spirit of faith—the spirit that took Joshua and Caleb to their destinies.

In Joshua 14:7-14, we see Caleb at eighty-five years old as he was possessing the Promised Land and fulfilling his destiny. He was still strong enough to defeat the giants and possess his mountain. He didn't settle for the wilderness; he didn't settle for a small farm in the valley; he didn't even settle for a piece of property on the Jordan River. He wanted the greatest mountain in the area, and he was going to build his house right on the top of it. The fact that there were many giants living on that mountain did not deter him. The fact that he was eighty-five years old and all his friends except Joshua had died didn't matter to him. He knew his destiny, and he had a spirit of faith. So he went after his mountain!

How many Christians settle for life in the wilderness, or life in the valley, when God has made available to them a mountaintop? They have a great destiny, but the spirit of fear or unbelief stops them from possessing it. They love the Lord, but they never see His full plan come to pass in their lives. To develop a spirit of faith, we must renew the spirit of our mind (Eph. 4:23). I won't elaborate on the details of this point, but realize that as you renew the spirit of your mind, you will see a different spirit begin to control your life. You will begin to possess the mountaintop, and you will not die in the wilderness. (See my book *Being Spiritually Minded* for more teaching on this subject.)

A spirit of faith will manifest itself with seven characteristics:

1. Those with a spirit of faith never just go along with the majority.
2. Those with a spirit of faith focus on God's promises, not on the giants.
3. Those with a spirit of faith speak of positive things, not negative ones.
4. Those who have a spirit of faith take risks others don't understand.

5. Those who have a spirit of faith befriend people with the same spirit.
6. Those who have a spirit of faith fight for excellence; they don't accept mediocrity.
7. Those with a spirit of faith fight to possess the mountain of destiny.

Handling Difficult Problems

As we walk our destiny course, we will face difficulties. Realize your destiny is worth it! Difficulties don't necessarily mean we've done something wrong or that we are off course. It's just part of living in a world that is still under the curse (Rom. 8:20-22). We must have the character and discipline to face the difficulties of the journey and not give up.

DESTINY KEY

YOUR DESTINY IS WORTH FIGHTING ALL ODDS, ALL ENEMIES, AND ALL CIRCUMSTANCES TO FULFILL.

Paul faced many problems and challenges as he fulfilled his destiny. Those who founded the great country of the United States fought terrible battles to give birth to a nation that was free, and many have fought since then to keep this nation free. The price was great. Realizing one's destiny isn't cheap, but it is the most rewarding experience you can imagine. The greater the enemy, the greater the victory. Only that which is valuable is worth fighting for. The fulfillment of your destiny is worth fighting all odds, all enemies, and all circumstances.

> *You therefore must endure hardship as a good soldier of Jesus Christ. No one engaged in warfare entangles himself with the affairs of this life, that he may please him who enlisted him as a soldier. And also if anyone competes in athletics, he is not crowned unless he competes according to the rules. The hardworking farmer must be first to partake of the crops. (2 Tim. 2:3-6)*

Hardships cannot be avoided, denied, or sidestepped. They must be *endured by faith.* The walk of destiny is not "a stroll in the park." If you are looking for an easy life, don't consider pursuing your destiny. God has a plan that will use all the gifts and talents you have. God will stretch you and maximize you to be all that you can be. He wants you to affect as many lives as possible and make as big a difference in this world as possible. You will have to rise higher than you ever thought you could. You will feel better about yourself than you ever have before.

> *But you be watchful in all things, endure afflictions, do the work of an evangelist, fulfill your ministry.* (2 Tim. 4:5)

Afflictions are the pressures and challenges of life—the relationship struggles, the financial pressures, and a host of other problems—that come at us as we walk our destiny path. While it is doubtful that we will ever face imprisonment, stonings, shipwrecks, and beatings as Paul did, nevertheless, we will be called to endure our own afflictions if we are to finish our course of destiny.

Have faith. Accept unflinchingly every hardship. You can handle people talking behind your back. You can take a setback at work without falling into self-pity. You can lose a loved one without losing your mind. Accept the challenges and problems and obstacles that go along with building the life God has called you to. It will not be an easy life. If you want "easy," then just get a job, make a living, pay the bills, and pray that Jesus returns quickly. But if you want to know your destiny, then get ready for the most exciting adventure that you could ever experience!

Five Faith-Filled Ways to Overcome Difficulties on Destiny's Course

As we walk the course of destiny in our lives, there are five things we must do to endure and overcome:

1. Through faith, stay focused on finishing the course.

In John 4, Jesus was weary and sat by a well to rest while the disciples went to get lunch. When the disciples returned and voiced concern about what Jesus would eat, He said to them, "I have food to eat of which you do not know. . . . My food is to do the will of Him who sent Me, and to finish His work" (John 4:32, 34). Jesus knew what His life's goal was, and He remained focused on it: to complete His destiny, "to finish His [the Father's] work."

We draw energy and sustenance from knowing by faith the destiny God has for us and from focusing by faith on finishing that work. Jesus said that His "food" was to do the will (fulfill the destiny) of God and finish His work—not to go halfway and quit, not to try it for a while and give up, not to get sidetracked into some worldly lifestyle, but to stay focused and finish the work—by faith.

2. By faith, don't delay seeking out your destiny.

Jesus gave some great insight for fulfilling our destiny and meeting the challenges that will come. He said:

> *"Do you not say, 'There are still four months and then comes the harvest'? Behold, I say to you, lift up your eyes and look at the fields, for they are already white for harvest!" (John 4:35)*

Excuses and procrastination have ravaged many people's destinies and kept many Christians from having God's best. The enemy will not say to you, "Don't do God's will." He will tell you, "Don't do God's will *today.*" If he can get you to wait, if he can get you to balk, one day at a time, then he can stop you forever.

Don't say you'll think about your destiny "in four months" or "when I get older" or "when I get out of school" or "when I can afford it" or "when I feel right about it." Jesus said, "Lift up your eyes *now* and see that the harvest is ready." Get on with it! Start where you are. Draw up your faith and get going! There will be many things that take time, and Jesus did say that you must count the cost. But there is something you can do right now to get

started with the pursuit of your destiny—something that God has put in your heart. By faith, do what you can now. Don't wait any longer.

Lift up your eyes! Get a vision! Don't *wait* for something to happen. In faith go *make* something happen. I like what one minister said years ago: "When the Lord puts something in your heart to do, do it quick before the devil convinces you that you can't do it."

3. Don't get entangled with the ways of the world.

To fight the battles that we will face, we cannot use the attitudes and methods of the world. We can't gossip, gripe, murmur, or waste our time watching Oprah, Donahue, and *As the World Turns.* We must live on a higher level and use spiritual weapons to win our battles. The world gets *bitter* about the things around them; we get *better.* The world *competes* with one another; we *complete* each other. The world points the finger of *blame;* we point to the *flame* of the Spirit of God, who can meet every need.

Because our enemy is not flesh and blood, we cannot face the challenges of life with mere human plans or weapons. Paul said:

> *For we do not wrestle against flesh and blood, but against principalities, against powers, against the rulers of the darkness of this age, against spiritual hosts of wickedness in the heavenly places. (Eph. 6:12)*

For centuries men have tried to solve their problems with laws, governments, and programs. These never work because the problems are spiritual, and natural weapons do not solve them. We must use spiritual weapons to deal with spiritual problems. Therefore we must not have the same attitudes that the world has—frustration, anxiety, anger, bitterness, and fear. We rise up in prayer—with love, faith, hope, and compassion—and we overcome the challenges that are before us.

As long as we walk in the Spirit and use spiritual forces to face problems, we will be successful. But when we get into the flesh

and begin to fight the same way people do in the natural world, we will be defeated and discouraged.

> *But if you bite and devour one another, beware lest you be consumed by one another! I say then: Walk in the Spirit.* (Gal. 5:15-16)

4. Keep a spirit of faith.

Remember how Paul faced being hard-pressed, perplexed, persecuted, and struck down? He kept a spirit of faith. It enabled him to look at things not seen and to not look at the things that were seen. He could see what the Lord was doing in the midst of trouble and keep on going after his destiny without being discouraged.

> *Therefore we do not lose heart. Even though our outward man is perishing, yet the inward man is being renewed day by day. For our light affliction, which is but for a moment, is working for us a far more exceeding and eternal weight of glory.* (2 Cor. 4:16-17)

The spirit of faith causes our inner man to rise up and walk on through the difficult times. If faith is just a doctrine or a message, we will forget it when things get tough and will not have the wherewithal to overcome. The spirit of faith causes us to talk right, walk right, and see right even when everything looks wrong.

Speak *to* the mountain, not *about* the mountain. Believe that God will enable you to move it. Get out of the boat and don't look at the wind or the waves. Keep your eyes on Jesus as you walk toward Him and the fulfillment of your destiny.

5. Face every hardship until you fulfill your destiny.

The Word is so clear in 2 Timothy 4:5. We are to stay cool and calm and accept the challenges that come without crying, whining, or shirking. When we try to live a life without struggles, we are actually avoiding our destiny path. In our world of get-rich-quick and get-ahead-quick schemes, where marriage and divorce are out of control, you and I must be different. We can't get

rid of every headache with a pill, and we can't solve every problem overnight. Liposuction isn't the way to lose weight, and 1-900-PSYCHIC isn't the place to find your destiny. Let's get down to the *discipline* of being disciples and facing the challenges that come to us with courage and character. Let's get in the Word; let's love each other; let's quit feeling sorry for ourselves; let's think about others instead of ourselves. Let's be like Jesus, seeking to do the Father's work to the end.

Most pastors leave the church they serve every four to five years. They don't have a commitment to their flock, and they don't have the endurance to handle the challenges of long-term relationships. That has brought about a type of church that views all ministries and commitments as short-term. That attitude flows over into family life, and many feel they can divorce and remarry whenever they feel like it. Because Christian leaders haven't faced challenges with endurance and faithfulness, many followers don't either.

The way to your destiny and fulfillment is to suffer unflinchingly every difficulty that comes along. Things will happen, circumstances will change, people will come and go, but your destiny doesn't change. What God has created you to do doesn't change. If you will stay on course, you will fulfill your destiny.

Steps to Your Destiny

1. Have you ever said, "If God wants it to happen, it will happen"? Maybe it's time for you to ask God for faith to reach out for His destiny plan for you.

2. Is your faith something you just have, or is it something you also do? In what area of your life can you begin acting out your faith more?

3. Have you renewed the spirit of your mind to have a spirit of faith? Only then can you possess the mountaintops.

4. Faith fights for victory. Do you believe fulfilling your God-given destiny is worth fighting all odds, all enemies, and all circumstances to fulfill?

5. Has your faith lost focus, delayed acting, or been polluted by the world? If so, write down what you can begin doing today to remedy that.

10

Following the Steps of Abraham

One of the greatest Bible heroes and men of faith was Abraham. He was the father of our faith, the founder of our covenant relationship with God. But Abraham's life was not a bed of roses, and fulfilling his destiny was not a cakewalk. In the following pages you will see events in Abraham's life that almost cost him his destiny. The wise things he did will encourage you to follow his example, while the foolish things he did will show you what *not* to do. That's one of the great things about the Bible. God doesn't just show us the good; He also shows us the bad. Let's learn from the faith of Abraham and the way he handled problems to make sure we too will fulfill our destiny.

Breaking the Parent Trap

Abraham's father, Terah, did not establish a great heritage of following God and being faithful in seeking his destiny. It seems he was one of those dads that had good intentions but didn't follow through. I'm sure he instilled some good things in his son's heart, but he also set some bad examples.

Genesis 11 tells us that Terah took Abraham and the rest of the family and left the land of Ur, a place known for its worship of the moon. Astrologers were the religious leaders there, and they

were caught up in the study of the zodiac and other forms of idolatry. Thank God Terah got Abraham out of that place! But Terah did not reach his destination, the land of Canaan. He stopped in Haran, which means "a dry, parched, burned-out place." If the name of the region has anything to do with the condition of Terah's life (and often it does in the Bible), then Terah burned out before he reached his destiny. He died in Haran.

How many Christians do you know who seemed to be on their way to a great destiny but then got stuck somewhere along the way? Some circumstance caused them to become angry, discouraged, or bitter, and before they knew it, they were burned out, dried up, and stuck in a parched life.

Years ago I knew a young man who felt called into the ministry and who came to our school. He was doing well, and we all recognized that he was a gifted individual. But then one day a challenge came along. A position that he had hoped to fill was taken by another, and there was no funding for an additional position at the time. He became a discouraged, angry, "dried up," and "burned-out" Christian. Proverbs 17:22 says, "A broken spirit dries the bones." The young man's attitude caused him to dry up spiritually and lose the vision that God had put in him. He allowed one obstacle to knock him off his course of destiny, and he has not recovered even today. While on your way to the promised land of destiny, don't get stuck in "Haran."

This was the example with which Abraham was raised. Many Christians cannot break free of the way their parents lived. They've been indoctrinated with the beliefs, attitudes, and lifestyle of a family whose members never sought their destinies. They let the traditions and the examples of their parents keep them from the promised land to which God has called them. Many think they should stay close to their relatives at all costs. But Jesus disputed that thinking:

> *"Do not think that I came to bring peace on earth. I did not come to bring peace but a sword. For I have come to 'set a man against his father, a daughter against her mother, and a daughter-in-law against her mother-in-law'; and 'a man's enemies will be those of his own household.' He who loves father or mother more than*

Me is not worthy of Me. And he who loves son or daughter more than Me is not worthy of Me." (Matt. 10:34-37)

Then His mother and brothers came to Him, and could not approach Him because of the crowd. And it was told Him by some, who said, "Your mother and Your brothers are standing outside, desiring to see You." But He answered and said to them, "My mother and My brothers are these who hear the word of God and do it." (Luke 8:19-21)

When family traditions are based on the Word, they are good in God's eyes. But when they are based on insecurities, control, fears, and sin, they must be left behind in "Ur." We must take the Word and the will of God for our lives above everything else. Honoring our father and mother is good, but that may not mean always *following* their examples or adopting their beliefs and attitudes.

Another aspect of this truth is that we must never let our family backgrounds limit our own future. The fact that one was born into a poor family doesn't have to mean anything about one's financial future. The fact that one was born into an abusive family doesn't have to mean anything about one's future relationships. The fact that your siblings constantly outdid you doesn't mean you have to outdo everyone else in your life. Alcoholism, drug use, emotional abuse, poverty—all these things are often passed on in a tradition of negativity. Rise to a higher level, and be all that God has created you to be, regardless of your family history.

DESTINY KEY

RISE TO A HIGHER LEVEL, AND BE ALL THAT GOD HAS CREATED YOU TO BE, REGARDLESS OF YOUR FAMILY HISTORY.

Abraham went on to the Promised Land and his destiny. No roots, family traditions, or even genetics could keep him from God's will for his life.

In my own family there are people who wish I was not a pastor, author, or teacher. They talk about me to others and shake their heads in disgust. Some relatives think of me as an embarrassment

to the family. They would rather I go back to the way I was raised—just make a living, be a nice guy, and try to get through life quietly. But the ways of my family and the way I was raised have nothing to do with the destiny God has for my life. I'm going on to the promised land with or without my relatives. If you have a great family heritage, wonderful! But if you don't, do as the apostle Paul said: "Leave it behind and press on to the high calling of God in Christ."

Don't let the way you were raised, the habits of your parents, or the attitudes of your family keep you from your promised land of destiny. Follow Abraham's example and break free.

Don't Carry Extra Baggage

When Abraham left Haran, he was breaking free of his father's burned-out life, but he made a mistake. God had already specifically told Abraham to get away from his family (Gen. 12:1). But Abraham decided to take along some excess baggage: his nephew Lot. (Bad decisions don't always look bad from the start.) Lot was not interested in pursuing God's destiny. He was along for the ride. He had no relationship with God. He had a personal agenda and a selfish motivation for being with Abraham, and soon there were problems:

> *Now the land was not able to support them, that they might dwell together, for their possessions were so great that they could not dwell together. And there was strife between the herdsmen of Abram's livestock and the herdsmen of Lot's livestock. (Gen. 13:6-7)*

The land would have been able to support Abraham, but he had disobeyed God's command and as a result he found himself in the midst of strife. By trying to keep this relationship, Abraham was opening his life to all kinds of evil. If God had wanted Lot to be with Abraham, the land would have supported both of them. God will provide more than enough when you follow His plan for your destiny.

Remember, Jesus said that your father, mother, sister, and brother are those who do the will of your heavenly Father. You

are not responsible for every person who wants to ride along with you. Although we are to love our families and care for and honor our parents, we are not to sacrifice the will of God or our destiny for them. In Abraham's case, he was commanded to leave his family, but instead he took them with him. It almost cost him everything.

The name *Lot* means "veil." To me it symbolizes the veiled or hidden agenda that Lot pursued—a personal agenda that was not based on God's will or destiny. When we allow friends or family to impose on us their own personal, hidden, or veiled agendas, it usually produces trouble. We must live for God and God's will, not the ambitions of others.

When you are on course with destiny and the blessing of God is flowing in your life, there will be many who would like to latch on to you. There is something about a person living within his or her destiny that attracts others. Sometimes it's good, if they come seeking the will of God in their own lives. But beware of those who come with hidden agendas. And remember what the Lord has said to you. If He said leave your father's house, make sure you leave, and don't take it with you.

DESTINY KEY

GUARD YOUR RELATIONSHIPS. THEY HAVE MUCH TO DO WITH YOUR DESTINY.

When the strife arose, Abraham had the wisdom to separate himself from its source. He told Lot to choose the land he wanted, and he would take the other. Lot moved toward Sodom and soon was caught up in the evil of that city. Later he was taken captive by kings from the north who came down to rob the king of Sodom. Abraham and his servants took it upon themselves to set Lot free. The Lord helped Abraham, and he was able to save the whole city. But again, we see the trouble Lot caused. Abraham paid a price for trying to keep the wrong relationships.

> *Do not be unequally yoked together with unbelievers. For what fellowship has righteousness with lawlessness? And what communion has light with darkness? (2 Cor. 6:14)*

Guard your relationships. They have much to do with your destiny. Don't be like Abraham and take the wrong people with you. But if you do, follow his example and separate yourself from them as soon as you can. It will cause some pain, but it may get you back on course with destiny.

Lies and Compromises

> *And it came to pass, when he was close to entering Egypt, that he said to Sarai his wife, "Indeed I know that you are a woman of beautiful countenance. Therefore it will happen, when the Egyptians see you, that they will say, 'This is his wife'; and they will kill me, but they will let you live. Please say you are my sister, that it may be well with me for your sake, and that I may live because of you."* (Gen. 12:11-13)

In this story, Abraham loses his integrity and reputation, and almost loses his wife. His compromises and lies jeopardized his future. He surely lost his influence with Egypt in terms of his godly example.

It's obvious that Abraham felt justified in his lie. We usually do. He thought he had good reasons for what he did, as we often think is the case when we lie. But the fact is, lies always open the door to the father of all lies, Satan. Whatever you hope to gain, you will lose. The world's way never works. God's way may seem difficult, but it is the only way. By taking the high road, you will find help from the Lord. By lying, you fall into Satan's trap.

Compromise is accepting less than you hoped for or doing what you do not believe in because you lack the courage to fight for what you do believe in. We *give up* and *give in,* then we think we will *get out* of the problem. But, in fact, we get in deeper. Abraham found himself in big trouble when the Egyptians took Sarah into Pharoah's house, and Pharaoh tried to keep her for himself. If it hadn't been for divine intervention, he could have lost his wife and the mother of his yet-to-be-born son. Through a dream, God spoke to Pharaoh, and he released Sarah to return to Abraham.

It could be that Abraham never should have gone to Egypt in the first place. It is not recorded that the Lord directed him there, and Egypt, being a symbol of the world, was a place that God's people were to avoid. By compromising and going to Egypt in the first place, Abraham set himself up for a series of compromises and lies that were dangerous to his future, his life, and his destiny. You can never tell just one lie. You inevitably find yourself telling more to cover the first.

DESTINY KEY

IN REACHING FOR YOUR DESTINY, KEEP HONESTY AND INTEGRITY CLOSE TO YOUR HEART.

The Lord got Abraham out of trouble because Abraham's heart and mind were set on following God and fulfilling his destiny, but the lesson is clear. Compromise and lies will never help you fulfill your destiny. They may even cost you your destiny. Most people don't fail because of outside attacks. They fail because of inner compromises. It's not deep wisdom we need to succeed in life. It is the basics like honesty and integrity. Integrity is a rare commodity these days. Not everyone has it. You would do well as you reach for your destiny to keep honesty and integrity close to your heart.

Willing to Fight for What Is Right

The kings of Chedorlaomer began to fight with those around them, and soon Sodom and Gomorrah fell. Lot, his family, and all his possessions were taken captive. Abraham didn't have to get involved. It wasn't his fight. He could have gone on about his business. But his character would not let him. He could not live as an island unto himself without regard for those around him. Unlike many in today's world, Abraham was one who did something. Genesis 14:14 says, "He armed his three hundred and eighteen trained servants who were born in his own house, and went in pursuit" to rescue Lot and his family.

In this story we see Abraham's concern for others and his willingness to sacrifice for them when there would be no benefit

to him personally. He did not have the "what's-in-it-for-me?" attitude that pervades society today. As you travel your destiny course, don't be the priest or the Levite, passing a needy person by as you travel life's road. Be a good Samaritan. Be selfless. Give someone your time; listen to their heartache; help them with their children; take them out to eat. Achieving your destiny means stopping along the way to help others, not barreling through your days like an uncaring Levite.

Sadly, coming to the aid of other human beings is not normal in our world. Americans spend more on dog food annually than they give to their church. Jesus said, "For where your treasure is, there your heart will be also" (Matt. 6:21). It appears we are closer to our dogs than we are to the Lord!

We also see that Abraham had resources to use for the support of others. It is God's will for you to have more than you need emotionally and materially. He wants you to have an abundance that will overflow to others. It may be that you will not be able to fulfill your destiny unless you have the resources to serve others and give beyond yourself.

Abraham went north, fought the kings who had taken Lot captive, and rescued the whole city. He had the wisdom and military savvy to pull it off, and he had the guts to go for it. Destiny doesn't just happen to us. We must have the wherewithal to go for it. God will always provide what we need, but we must use what we have for Him. If we don't do our part, why should we expect God to do His? Abraham had the people, weapons, leadership skills, and courage to try to save the two cities. As he walked with God and stayed on course, Abraham was becoming a man of destiny.

Knowing the Possessor of Heaven and Earth

One of the things we see clearly about Abraham is that he was a prosperous man. As he walked with God, God blessed him with livestock, silver, and gold (Gen. 13:2). He had more than three hundred servants who had been born in his house (Gen. 14:14). That means almost a thousand people were involved with Abraham's business and family.

There were no Old Testament laws and no spiritual requirements established by God at this point, but Abraham still was a giver. When Abraham came back from defeating the kings and freeing Lot, he met Melchizedek, who was a priest and the king of Salem. Genesis 14:20 says, "And he [Abraham] gave him a tithe of all." Now Melchizedek is a symbolic representation of Jesus, the Head of the Church, the Prince of Peace. Without requirement from the law (it came 430 years later), without a sermon on giving, and without outward provocation, Abraham gave. A tenth was a significant amount in a wealthy man like Abraham's case, but he gave it freely. Genesis 14:22-23 tells us how and why Abraham gave as he did:

"I have raised my hand to the LORD." Abraham had a covenant and a relationship with the Lord. He knew and trusted God. His wasn't a dead religion. It wasn't merely a tradition. It was real, a covenant that he would not dishonor or break.

". . . God Most High . . . ." The Lord was the top priority in Abraham's life. He didn't have God down the list somewhere between the house, the job, and the boat. He served God as the "Most High"; there was nothing higher in his life. So often we put God after our career, recreation, family, or personal ambitions. Abraham said, He is "God Most High."

DESTINY KEY

YOU WILL BE ONE STEP FARTHER DOWN THE ROAD TO YOUR DESTINY WHEN YOU LEARN TO BE A FAITHFUL TITHER AND GIVER.

". . . the Possessor of heaven and earth." Abraham knew the source of everything. His sheep, the grass they ate, the fields they roamed, the water they drank, all came from God. He is still the Possessor of heaven and earth. You and I are just squatters. We don't own the earth, and we can't take it with us. Although we may act possessive and give nothing to the "Landlord," it is still His. When you really know that God is the owner of all you have, it's easy to tithe.

The struggle many have with giving comes from their misconception of the world we live in. They think *they* are making a living and making their own way. Thinking we own our life and

the things around us causes us to be greedy and materialistic. "The earth is the LORD'S, and all its fullness" (Ps. 24:1). Remembering this and living as though it's true will make you more like Abraham. When you are a generous giver—of your time, your love, your talents, your wisdom, and your money—God will likely trust you with more resources and bless you in a greater way. But if you are miserly with what you have, why should God increase it?

The prophet Malachi said:

"You are cursed with a curse,
For you have robbed Me,
Even this whole nation.
Bring all the tithes into the storehouse,
That there may be food in My house,
And try Me now in this,"
Says the LORD of hosts,
"If I will not open for you the windows of heaven
And pour out for you such blessing
That there will not be room enough to receive it." (Mal. 3:9-10)

Tithing of all our resources—spiritual, emotional, and physical—is basic to Christianity. It honors God and shows that we know Him as Lord. He is the Source, the Owner, and the Provider. When we give at least one-tenth of our income, we open our lives to receive His blessing. There will always be those who argue about giving, but their motive is usually selfishness, fear, or unbelief, and the results can usually be seen in the lack and shortage in their lives. Follow the giving of Abraham, and you will prosper. You will be one step farther down the road to your destiny when you learn to be a faithful tither and giver.

The Lasting Consequences of Sin

In Genesis 16, Abraham made what may be the biggest mistake of his life. It brought him great grief and almost cost him his destiny. After waiting for years to have a child, Sarah, Abraham's wife, became impatient. She did not have the kind of relationship

with the Lord that Abraham had. She walked with Abraham but didn't really walk with God. Because of this weak relationship, she pushed her husband to do something that would hurt their marriage, their family, and their future. She talked Abraham into having sex with her maid, Hagar, so she and Abraham could have a child. Abraham didn't argue, and soon Hagar was pregnant. It wasn't long before strife entered the house. Sarah was jealous of Hagar's child, and Hagar used the child to rise above her servanthood. The child, Ishmael, became a source of conflict among Sarah, Abraham, and Hagar.

Finally Sarah became pregnant. Isaac caused even more conflict between Sarah and Hagar. Sarah pressed Abraham to kick out Hagar and Ishmael, who was now a teenager. After much turmoil, Abraham did as Sarah asked. God blessed the child Ishmael because he had come from Abraham, but he was not the child that God would use to bless the world. He was not the fulfillment of Abraham's destiny.

Ishmael's descendants became the Arab nations and the source of the Moslem faith. Because of Abraham's sin, Israel has struggled in war for centuries. The pain and problems that Abraham brought upon himself and his people through Ishmael's birth seem endless.

How many of us have done things we wish we could undo? Adultery, divorce, compromise, or some other sin can be forgiven, but its consequences often have a high cost. Though we are forgiven for the sin, we can't undo its consequences. God forgave Abraham, and he went on to fulfill his destiny, but the consequences were still there.

If we will use our ability to look ahead and see the results our choices are likely to bring, we will not get caught in such circumstances. It seemed that at an early age in the Lord, I was able to look ahead at the consequences of my choices and make the right ones. While in drug rehabilitation, I saw dozens of people leave the program and return to their old lifestyles. They always believed things would be different, and they could avoid the problems of their past. But they never did. It may be that their destiny in the Lord was forfeited because of those choices. I'm sure there are some who will never rise to what they could have been in God had they stayed right with Him.

When opportunities to compromise or rationalize the truth came, I stayed on course with God's help, because I could see the potential bad consequences. I thank God for that, because it has kept me free from untold problems throughout my years as a Christian. Wendy and I know the joy of being able to say we didn't have sex before we were married. We can tell our children how we dated and how to build a solid foundation for marriage. I can look back with thankfulness and satisfaction that I have never "backslidden" since the day I was saved. Not one drink of alcohol or illegal drug has touched my lips since I was born again. Not one other woman has been in my life since Jesus and Wendy came in. To some this may mean nothing, but to me all this is evidence of a strong relationship with God and an ability to look ahead at the consequences that every decision brings.

Abraham paid for years for the time he spent with Hagar. How many people do we know who pay their whole lives for the sin of one night or one decision? To lose your spouse, children, and testimony for short-term pleasure doesn't make sense. It never brings a better life, and the pain of those choices is often long-term. Let's learn from Abraham. No matter who encourages us to go to "Hagar," let's not. "Isaac," the child of the promise, is worth the wait. The consequences that never go away and constantly hinder our pursuit of destiny are just not worth it.

On the other hand, the results of spirit-led choices that were part of our destiny never bring remorse. They bring God's blessings and the fulfillment of destiny into our lives. Keep your eyes down the road of life. Always consider the consequences of your actions.

Standing in the Gap

For anyone to accomplish a great destiny in God, he or she must have great heart. Genesis 18 shows the heart of Abraham toward the Lord and all people. His strength and dedication make it clear why he was chosen by the Lord for such a significant role in human history.

The story begins with the Lord coming to Abraham and talking personally with him about His promises. Then the Lord turns toward Sodom and Gomorrah to see if the wickedness of these cities is really true. Before He leaves, the Lord turns back to Abraham and says:

> *"Shall I hide from Abraham what I am doing? . . . For I have known him, in order that he may command his children and his household after him, that they keep the way of the LORD, to do righteousness and justice, that the LORD may bring to Abraham what He has spoken to him." (Gen. 18:17-19)*

DESTINY KEY

DON'T LET THE FULFILLMENT OF DESTINY OR PROSPERITY IN YOUR LIFE DIE WITH YOU; PASS THE BATON TO THE NEXT GENERATION.

Notice that God desires to share His plans with Abraham because He knows Abraham has a heart to fulfill his destiny and build a great nation. He also knows that Abraham will command his children to follow God. This is one of the signs of greatness, families that serve the Lord generation after generation.

We must not live for our generation only. We must look farther down the road and prepare for future generations by raising our children properly. We must put a sense of destiny into their hearts—and the vision and discipline that go with it. Don't let the call of destiny die with you; pass it to the next generation. There is no reason why our descendants should have to start at the bottom again. Let's help them start where we finish and rise even higher. We can teach them the discipline they need to appreciate and use their resources wisely. We can teach them to live by the spirit of faith. Let's be like Abraham and pass on a sense of destiny to our children and their children and see the great plan of God go on for generations.

God tells Abraham that He plans to judge and destroy Sodom and Gomorrah for their wickedness. These two cities were con-

sumed in evil, drunkenness, reveling, and homosexuality. Abraham could have been like many Christians today and just agreed with the Lord to see the destruction of wickedness. He could have said, "I knew it would happen. Those people deserve the judgment of God that they have received." But Abraham had a more loving heart than that.

He stood before the Lord and began to intercede on their behalf. He stood in the gap for them and challenged the Lord about His plan. "Suppose there were fifty righteous within the city; would You . . . spare it?" (Gen. 18:24) he asked. He then negotiated God down to ten righteous. It wasn't difficult to get God to agree, because He is quick to be merciful. The courage Abraham showed to stand before the Lord and the love he showed to intercede for a wicked people were evidence of the heart of a great man with a great sense of destiny.

We in the church must learn from Abraham's example. Our traditional way is to preach to sinners and act like we hate them. The people outside the church feel condemned and despised by us, not loved. They assume we don't like them, so why should they come to our church? Even if they want God, they don't feel like they could come to us for help finding Him. We must turn this around. Though we will never agree with their lifestyles, we are to love sinners and invite them into our world. We want them to be saved and to find their destiny in God. We are not here to condemn and judge but to love and save. Let's get the heart of Abraham, one that intercedes for and believes in sinners' salvation and doesn't rejoice over their judgment.

Willing to Relinquish Everything

In Genesis 22, Abraham faced the biggest challenge of his lifetime. After twenty-five years of waiting and walking with God, Abraham saw the birth of Isaac, the promised son of destiny. This was the boy who would lead the family to become a mighty nation, God's nation, out of which the Messiah, the Savior of the world, would come. Born to a ninety-year-old woman and a one-hundred-year-old man, Isaac was a miracle. Now came the ultimate test.

God asked Abraham to sacrifice the boy, who was about seventeen years old, as a burnt offering. I'm not sure if Abraham hesitated or not. It appears in Genesis 22 that he had come to a place of maturity in the Lord where he immediately responded to this command with obedience. Hebrews 11:19 says that Abraham believed God would raise Isaac from the dead, so he planned to go all the way with sacrificing his only son from Sarah. He had already given up Ishmael, his son by Hagar, because of problems in the home. Now he was going to have to give up Isaac, the promised son.

Apparently he didn't hesitate but packed his donkey and headed to the mount with the wood and torch he needed to build a fire. When Isaac saw the wood and the torch, he asked his dad where the lamb for sacrifice was. His father responded, "The Lord will provide the lamb." Upon reaching the appropriate spot, Abraham bound his son and raised the knife to kill him. But the angel of the Lord stopped him at the last second and said:

> *"Do not lay your hand on the lad, or do anything to him; for now I know that you fear God, since you have not withheld your son, your only son, from Me." (Gen. 22:12)*

God had placed a ram in the bushes, and Abraham sacrificed the ram to the Lord. His commitment had met the ultimate test. He was willing to relinquish the most valuable thing in his life for the fulfillment of his destiny. You and I will not be called upon to sacrifice our children, but there will be tests along the way to our destiny. Are we willing to relinquish the most valuable thing in our lives? Maybe it's our career, our title, or our office. Maybe it's our image or our place in society. Maybe it's the material possessions we prize and admire.

A few years ago I heard the story of Bruce Kennedy, who was the highly successful president of Alaska Airlines. After bringing this company to a place of prominence and prosperity, he resigned. In itself that is not uncommon for CEOs. They seem to come and go quite regularly. But the thing he left it for was astounding to many. He wasn't going to another company to accept the challenge of leadership and to turn it around for profit's sake. He wasn't

moving on to a bigger and better position, office, or salary. He was going to the mission field to serve the Lord.

The normal executive could not understand Kennedy's decision to leave so much behind for a mission compound and the chance to serve a few Chinese people. I haven't heard the end of the story yet, but I'm sure a great destiny is being fulfilled by a man who took the ultimate test and sacrificed it all. (An interesting footnote to this story is that several key Christian Faith Center employees came out of Alaska Airlines while Bruce Kennedy was still president. His influence has been significant.)

What if Abraham had said no to the Lord? Feeling totally justified, he could have said, "God, I've given enough. I've served you for twenty-five years. I've gone through trial and tribulation for this child, and I'm not giving him up." His response would have been very normal, and none of us could have faulted him for it. But Abraham lived for a higher purpose, a higher calling. Destiny rang in his ears, so the sacrifice would be performed, because it was another step to the fulfillment of God's destiny will and plan.

DESTINY KEY

THE SOONER YOU DEVELOP STRONG FAITH IN GOD, THE SOONER YOU WILL TRAVEL THE ROAD TO YOUR DESTINY.

Many have asked me through the years why I go through the challenges of building a college or media ministry. It would be easy to kick back and enjoy a nice salary from a nice church, they reason. But I hear the call of destiny in my spirit. To be comfortable or successful in the eyes of the world holds no satisfaction. To fulfill my destiny and hear the Lord say, "Well done, good and faithful servant," is the reason I live, and the reason I lay it all on the altar of sacrifice. It's all God's anyway, so what have I got to lose?

The Key to It All

Abraham's life is a great example of a man who walked with God and fulfilled his destiny. He didn't do everything right, but

the grace and the mercy of God brought him through. The one thing Abraham did in every situation that may be the key to it all was this: He believed God.

Abraham had the key of faith working in his life. Faith in God is the only hope for realizing your destiny. Romans 4 says:

> *Abraham believed God, and it was accounted to him for righteousness. (v. 3)*

> *For the promise that he would be the heir of the world was not to Abraham or to his seed thorough the law, but through the righteousness of faith. (v. 13)*

> *[Abraham] Who, contrary to hope, in hope believed, so that he became the father of many nations, according to what was spoken, "So shall your descendants be." And not being weak in faith, he did not consider his own body, already dead (since he was about a hundred years old), and the deadness of Sarah's womb. He did not waver at the promise of God through unbelief, but was strengthened in faith, giving glory to God, and being fully convinced that what He had promised He was also able to perform. (vv. 18-21)*

As I've shown in previous chapters, we must live by faith, walk by faith, and fight the fight of faith. We can never stray away from the faith-filled life if we desire to fulfill our destiny. The sooner you develop strong faith in God, the sooner you will get down the road to your destiny. I pray that the life of Abraham will inspire you to greatness and to a great destiny.

Steps to Your Destiny

1. In seeking to fulfill your destiny, what can you learn from the faith of Abraham and the way he handled problems?

2. Abraham went toward his destiny no matter what anyone else did. Are there people from whom you need to separate so you can continue on destiny's course?

3. Compromise is accepting less than you hoped for or doing what you do not believe in because you lack the courage to fight. Are there areas of compromise in your life right now?

4. Abraham was a giver! What possessions, dreams, or gifts do you need to give back to God today?

11

Putting It All Together

In this last chapter we will tie together the key ingredients we've considered so far. To begin, let's review some key terms we've discussed in these pages:

- *Destiny:* A course or path in life that includes both the God-given destination you are seeking at life's end and your own faith-filled journey toward that destination.
- *Vision:* The ability to anticipate, imagine, or foresee experiences and developments to participate in or avoid as you travel destiny's course.
- *Calling:* The specific thing you do—a career or job or ministry in which God has placed you as you seek to accomplish a purpose, fulfill a vision, and complete your course of destiny.
- *Purpose:* The reason you do what you do.
- *Goals:* Specific skills, accomplishments, and events (mileposts on destiny's course) that you desire to achieve.
- *Plan:* This is a new one. Your plan is a written series of hoped-for events and accomplishments that

coincides with your goals, calling, purpose, and vision as you travel your destiny path.

Everything flows from your sense of destiny. Ephesians 2:10 says:

For we are His workmanship, created in Christ Jesus for good works, which God prepared beforehand that we should walk in them.

Out of a sense of destiny comes vision, purpose, calling, goals, and plans. If you have made it this far in this book and applied its concepts to any degree, I'm sure you have a sense of God's destiny for your life. Now let's return to my testimony and see how, once I discovered that God had a destiny for me (as I pray that you now have), I began to act in vision, with purpose, out of calling, in keeping with my goals, and with a plan.

In January of 1976, about a year after I'd been born again, I entered a small Bible school in Seattle. I had a desire to help people and serve the Lord. Out of that desire came motivation to prepare myself for service and to sort out my destiny—to minister the gospel to as many people as the Lord would let me. I didn't have it all together when I started, but I was going with the desire I felt to do this. (Remember, God-given and God-directed desires are good.) My pastor, Art Sather, had given me a wise bit of counsel: "You can't steer a bike until it's rolling." I started the bike rolling as I entered ministry school.

At the same time, I was active in my local church. I taught the Royal Rangers children's club every Wednesday evening. I ushered every service, attended the pastor's Sunday school class, and helped clean up after each baptism. I was excited and looked for ways to get involved with the work of the Lord. After Wendy and I started dating during the second month of school, we taught the junior-high class every Sunday and Wednesday. That class, which had sixteen children our first week, had more than fifty kids a few months later.

I became the assistant director at the Washington Drug Rehabilitation Center after graduating from the program. That meant that I was in group therapy sessions around the city about four evenings a week and involved with daily counseling as well as

leadership of the program staff and residents. Between school, church, and WDRC, we had a busy life. We were stretching out in faith, yet we also were trying to be patient and let God reveal His plan in His own time.

It was from this place of study and ministry and faith that Wendy and I began to discover our destiny as ministers. You can't set your course with God from an easy chair. You will not hear the Word of the Lord for your life in a sit-com. You can't steer a bike until it is rolling. Boy, were we rolling!

Those were exciting days for Wendy and me. We were learning from the junior-high kids and the WDRC residents and helping in all kinds of services and activities. Trying things like leadership seminars, self-help workshops, and special programs helped us grow and learn dramatically. We were developing and discovering at the same time. As we explored our destiny as ministers of the gospel, we began to develop a *vision* to lead a church and ministry. The vision flowed from our sense of destiny. We didn't know it at the time, but this was the foundation for Christian Faith Center and everything we are doing today. Without those developmental years, we would never have found our destiny or built our vision for ministry.

As you develop a vision (with the input of others), it's a good idea to write it down. Then you will always have it to refer to.

> *Then the LORD answered me and said: "Write the vision and make it plain on tablets, that he may run who reads it. For the vision is yet for an appointed time; but at the end it will speak, and it will not lie. Though it tarries, wait for it; because it will surely come, it will not tarry." (Hab. 2:2-3)*

Too many people are waiting for something to happen before they follow their desires and destiny. They want a solid direction and a settled destination before they get going. God may give you your vision in increments. In that sense you need to exercise patience. But He will always require that you get out of the boat with faith and dedicate yourself to learning and growing before He will bring you to a sense of destiny.

"Many are called, but few chosen" (Matt. 20:16). I'm convinced this is true, because most people will not go through the devel-

opmental process to find and fulfill their calling in destiny. Some even catch a glimpse of their destiny and a part of a vision, but they don't act on it enough to seek out their calling.

During the years of school and volunteer service, I was acting on my sense of destiny and vision as I received it. This was a time of experimenting, of discovering what I wanted to do and what I didn't want to do, what I was good at and what I wasn't good at. My calling was coming into focus.

At first I thought I would be a counselor, probation officer, or something like that. I figured I could help people with problems and teach them how to overcome. In the second year of school, I began to feel a desire and sense an ability to teach the Word. I thought maybe I could be an associate pastor and help on the staff of a church. I could serve in various ways and be a good support man to a senior pastor. I was even asked to be a deacon at our church that year, but the elders withdrew the invitation because some of the members thought I was too young.

All this time Wendy and I were faithful in our Sunday and Wednesday class with the young people. We led several groups a week and counseled many people. I was still in school. At times we were exhausted, but we know you don't find destiny by saying you're too tired to help with the children's ministry or usher on Wednesday night.

In the third year of school I began to watch evangelist Fred Price on TV. Sunday nights I would race home from whatever church I was speaking in (about the work of WDRC) just in time to watch Dr. Price. My best friend, Julius Young (the founder of WDRC), and I would listen raptly to Dr. Price's messages and rejoice in his fresh style and delivery. I never heard anything from Dr. Price that we didn't believe at our church and Bible school. The only difference was that Dr. Price taught that it would work *right now!* Rather than just "hoping and praying," I could pray and *believe,* and things would happen. This new understanding of faith radically affected my vision. I realized how small-minded I had been and how I had failed to believe God for everything in my life.

I began to memorize Scripture with greater zeal than I ever had. My papers at school took on a new spirit of faith, and I began to see the Lord doing more in my life than ever before. I could

see myself as a pastor of a church with maybe five hundred members. (My destiny of ministry was the same, but my vision was expanding.) I began to hold leadership training classes with my friends in WDRC, and we started building our leadership skills.

In the fall of 1979, out of a sense of destiny and a growing vision, the call of God to be a senior pastor was clarified in my heart. That was my *calling*—the career in which I would work to fulfill my destiny as a minister and my vision as a leader of God's people. I could no longer see myself doing anything else but pastoring a church. No other option attracted me. I began to focus on being a senior leader.

A few opportunities to serve on a church staff came along. One group wanted Wendy and me to take over their church, and a denomination asked us to pastor a church in their group. Wendy and I thought and prayed about these things, but we never felt a witness from the Lord that it was the direction for us.

Finally in November of 1979, I went to my pastor and told him I wanted to start a church. To my delight, he supported my decision. This is a very important point. If my pastor had told me I should wait, I would have waited. I was ready to do whatever he counseled me to do. After several meetings with my pastor and the board, Wendy and I decided we would set out on our own. The church sent us out with its blessing. There was no financial support, but we had a great Sunday evening send-off service. We were on our way.

It is important to start with the blessing of your church leaders. If I had left the church in rebellion, I would have started CFC with that kind of spirit. Ed Cole teaches that the way you leave is the way you enter. Many people leave a ministry angry and hurt, and they enter their next ministry in the same spirit. Then when it fails, they can't understand why.

I remember driving down I-5 with Pastor Sather and saying to him as we drove past Sea-Tac in south Seattle, "I feel the Lord wants us to start in this area." He bore witness to the idea, and that was my green light. I looked throughout the area for a community center or hall to rent. I suddenly had an immediate purpose—to minister to a particular area and raise up a church there.

We needed a place to meet. I set that as a goal: I'd find us a building in which to hold church. I soon discovered a Christian school with a large gym that would seat a thousand people and a foyer that would seat two hundred. There were several classrooms, and there was room to park. I felt it was the place for us to begin services for Christian Faith Center. With my vision I could see the room filled. That became my next goal. I actually had flyers printed and began spreading them around before we had a final approval from the school board! I had goals for filling that place! I was either young and naive or led by the Lord with a spirit of faith (maybe both).

I finished ministry school in mid-December, and we had our first Sunday morning service on January 6, 1980. That first Sunday we had elders in office, children's leaders in classrooms, and a worship team ready to go. These people had participated in the Bible studies, seminars, and classes I'd taught for the previous two years. We had developed a plan. We had drawn our people together, and we knew what we wanted to do in each area of the church. We knew how we wanted the service to run, how we wanted to greet visitors, what kind of music we wanted, and how the Sunday school should be run. We had planned everything.

In May of 1980, Wendy and I visited Crenshaw Christian Center in California and received great input from Dr. Price for nearly a week. In July of 1980, we were ordained at Crenshaw. Our relationship with Dr. Price has continued to be invaluable. You become like the people with whom you fellowship. Align yourself with people who are going somewhere if you want to go somewhere.

As the days and months went by, my vision for the church grew. (As you walk your destiny course, your vision will inevitably expand and clarify.) Soon we began to envision a media ministry, missions, and teaching seminars in our (destiny) future. In the second year of the church, we went on television. In 1982 we bought ten acres of land. In 1983 we moved into our present sanctuary, which seats 2,500 people. Each year the properties have been expanded and ministries added to the church. Schools, a college, a bookstore, a restaurant, and a counseling center—all these things were the outgrowths of God's original destiny plan for my life: to reach and minister to as many as possible. As we

go on, I continue to revise and expand my goals and plans to perform my calling, achieve my purpose, and fulfill my destiny.

We started the church with a vision of building the Sunday services to one thousand people someday. We soon outgrew the little foyer that we were renting on Sundays and Wednesdays and moved into the gymnasium. In our second year, our services numbered about five hundred people, and we realized that our goal was coming to pass sooner than we had originally thought. Our vision of ministry quickly expanded. That meant making new plans, setting new goals. I began to plan for a second service. I looked at the schedule other churches used and how they were making it work. I took into consideration how it would affect our workers and volunteers. I planned the appropriate leadership and communication steps with the congregation. All this happened with the input and counsel of Wendy and our other leaders. We never considered *not* doing it—not growing, not changing, not moving on in growth and vision. Growth was one of our goals. It was not an option.

During that time we also continued planning the design for our own building. We had purchased ten acres, established a basic design, and started construction with the little money we had saved. We were about $500,000 into the project when it seemed we could go no further. We had spent all we had and needed another $1.5 million to complete the building. I started going to banks to see what money was available.

I've always operated under the philosophy of going as far as you can with what you have before borrowing. If the Lord brings the finances to finish, great. If not, look at other options. I leave a lot of room for miracles to see me through. While I am very specific in financial plans and budgets, I never want to limit God or predict what will come to pass. "A man's heart plans his way, but the LORD directs his steps" (Prov. 16:9).

"Unless the LORD builds the house, they labor in vain who build it" (Ps. 127:1). Some leaders would be nervous with my style, but I have always walked and lived by faith. We have never had large financial reserves in place before we stepped out to build or expand. At the same time, we know exactly where we are, how much money we think we can raise, and what we will do if our current plan doesn't get us to the finish line. I want to

be moving with a clear plan that demonstrates faith yet has alternatives in case the original plan doesn't work.

You can see that we have constantly planned and revised our plans. It's something you'll do until you reach the end of your destiny course. At the planning stage in your destiny course, write down the specific things you will do and when you plan to do them. Count the cost to finish.

> *"For which of you, intending to build a tower, does not sit down first and count the cost, whether he has enough to finish it—lest, after he has laid the foundation, and is not able to finish, all who see it begin to mock him, saying, 'This man began to build and was not able to finish.'"* (Luke 14:28-30)

Seven Tips for Power Planning

Use all your gifts, talents, knowledge, relationships, and spiritual abilities to establish the goals on your destiny course for success. Then follow these tips for *power planning*.

1. Start with a faith-filled, positive determination to succeed.

What you are decides what you will accomplish. You must *be* before you can *do*. The Lord said to Joshua, "Be strong and very courageous, that you may observe to do according to all the law which Moses My servant commanded you" (Josh. 1:7). I have spent years working on myself, and I still do. The successful ministry, the good family, the prosperous business, and the effective relationships flow out of the person. Get yourself together, and you will get your ministry or family or business or relationships together.

You must have a spirit of faith and optimism if you want to build anything or change the world. Everything will be against you at one time or another. Anything less than a total commitment to success will fall short, and you'll quit or become distracted. The runner must start with the finish line in mind. The halfback doesn't hope for three yards and a cloud of dust; he wants a touchdown. The builder starts with a blueprint, a picture

of the house. Start with your finished product, ministry, or business in mind.

2. Get the facts.

Know what you are up against and what must be done to succeed. Too many folks start with a naive view or inadequate knowledge. Hosea 4:6 says, "My people are destroyed for lack of knowledge." Get the facts, stay abreast of trends, and know what you are doing, whether you are building a business, starting college, opening a day-care center, or beginning a Bible study. Many people "spiritualize" what they are doing to the point that they fail to be practical. Be aware of reality. Ask:

- Who are your customers, clients, members, or participants?
- What are they looking for?
- What do they need?
- How can you better serve them?

Don't allow guesses and hunches to blind you to the facts. Proverbs 24:3-4 says:

Through wisdom a house is built,
And by understanding it is established;
By knowledge the rooms are filled.

3. Develop a step-by-step plan.

Write out the steps you must take to succeed, and prioritize them. Learn to think in an orderly manner and to plan linearly. That may be one of the strengths that has helped me most—the ability to think in an orderly manner, to see the necessary steps, and put the plan together. Any leader has to be able to think linearly.

Jesus had a great plan as He moved toward His destiny, the cross. First He called twelve leaders to follow Him and be trained. He then called seventy to spread the message of the kingdom and sow seeds that would grow after His death and resurrection. Finally He prepared His team for the last days of

His ministry and waited for the events to fall into place. It worked just as He and the Father had planned. Had Satan known the outcome, he would never have crucified the Lord of glory (1 Cor. 2:8).

4. Write down your power plan and your "what if" plan.

Plan to win, but be ready for setbacks or problems. In Luke 14:31-32, Jesus teaches us to be ready to negotiate if it's unlikely we'll win the war. What some people call faith is actually foolishness and/or a lack of preparation. It's not unbelief to say we need to devise alternative plans. Wisdom includes exploring your options and being flexible when necessary.

5. Revise the plan as your goals or circumstances change.

The ability to lead others through change or transitions is invaluable. You must not just endure change. You must lead through it, whether it's affecting your family, a business, a ministry, or simply your own life. Times change, seasons change, circumstances change, people change. The only thing that is constant, apart from God, is change. A great leader takes change in stride and leads himself and others through it. Don't solidify your plans to such a degree that you can never change. Have commitment, stability, and clarity, but use "erasable" stones for all your plans.

6. Surround yourself with wise people.

> *In the multitude of counselors there is safety. (Prov. 11:14)*

> *He who walks with wise men will be wise,*
> *But the companion of fools will be destroyed. (Prov. 13:20)*

These are truths every leader must remember. You can never get so big or be so successful that you don't need counselors, friends, and wise people around you. In fact, when you isolate yourself, you become a fool and rage against all wise judgment (Prov. 18:1-2). Hire people who can give you wise input, and stay in touch with those who give you honest counsel. I have three levels of people on my board of directors.

I listen to these and other associates whenever I face a major decision. Building a building, buying land, going on TV, starting a new department—none of these things happen without the input of my team.

7. Stay at it!

Nothing great happens quickly. The kingdom is like a seed that grows slowly and purposefully. So is any godly enterprise you pursue. Plants that spring up too quickly are usually spindly, weak, and unable to survive harsh winds. Though I often feel things are happening too slowly, I also realize that we're in this for the long haul. I don't have anything else to do or anywhere else to go, so I'll try to be patient until we get there. Great churches, businesses, families, and people are built only through patience and commitment.

My point in sharing my testimony has been to show you the progression of developing and discovering the destiny God has for you. You don't just get a "word" from the Lord and go off to do your thing. The unfolding of our destiny takes time, counsel, patience, prayer, and hard work. You will eventually discern your *destiny:* God will surely show it to you if you seek it. After discerning your destiny, you will begin to have *vision;* from that you'll either discern a new *calling* or confirm your present one; you'll suddenly have new *purpose;* and then you can *plan* how to reach the appropriate *goals*.

The destiny of the Lord grows in your life, "First the blade, then the head, after that the full grain" (Mark 4:28). As you give yourself to service, the Lord will make it clear to you. Take your time, give yourself to your tasks and to the Lord, and your destiny course will come into focus.

Steps to Your Destiny

1. What is the one thing you desire to see happen through you in the world? This may be your destiny.

2. Can you see any specific ways of making this happen? This may be part of your vision.

3. When you see yourself making this thing happen, what are you doing? This may be your calling.

4. What immediate action should you take to get on with your destiny? This may be your purpose.

5. As you define your purpose, what are the first steps you can take to achieve it? These are goals.

6. How can you achieve those goals? This involves planning. Use my tips to get yourself on the way to reaching your goals, meeting your purpose, enjoying your calling, realizing your vision, and fulfilling your destiny.

[illegible] of my closest and most trusted friends.
[illegible] Destiny comes straight from the heart
[illegible] d it deeply moves me. Read this book, and
[illegible] d-given destiny, its costs, and its rewards

Casey Treat is one
Fulfilling Your God-
and God's Word, an
better know your G

Oral Roberts
Tulsa, Oklahoma

Pastor Casey Treat has a compassionate heart for the needs of people from all walks of life. *Fulfilling Your God-Given Destiny* is a timely book. Today's Christians live in a whirlwind of activities, yet they desire peace and fulfillment in their lives. This book is a must for every believer.

Dr. David Yonggi Cho
Senior Pastor, Yoido Full Gospel Church, Seoul, Korea

Not only is Casey Treat a very close friend in the ministry, but I have come to regard him as one of the finest young Christian leaders in the body of Christ. His leadership skills and the fruit of his ministry are simply outstanding. This book will give you insight into the foundation and principles that have caused him to accomplish this in Christ Jesus.

Rev. Ray McCauley
Johannesburg, South Africa

Casey Treat is the most focused man I have met and the most unselfish. The simple and profound priciples in these chapters have changed not only my life, but the lives of thousands around the world, and they will change you. Get ready to move forward from an existence and "get-by" mentality to becoming a world changer.

Rick Godwin
Senior Minister, Eagle's Nest Christian Fellowship